W9-CLX-517

NIGHT

WITH A PERFECT

STRANGER

NIGHT

WITH A PERFECT

STRANGER

The Conversation That Changes Everything

DAVID GREGORY

WORTHY
PUBLISHING

Published by Worthy Publishing, a division of Worthy Media, Inc., 134 Franklin Road, Suite 200, Brentwood, Tennessee 37027.

HELPING PEOPLE EXPERIENCE THE HEART OF GOD

eBook available at www.worthypublishing.com

Audio distributed through Oasis Audio; visit www.oasisaudio.com

Library of Congress Control Number: 2011942287

For foreign and subsidiary rights, contact Riggins International Rights Services, Inc.; www.rigginsrights.com

The author is represented by MacGregor Literary, Inc., Hillsboro, Oregon.

ISBN: 978-1-936034-86-4 (hardcover w/ jacket)

Cover Image: © Shutterstock #25364728
Interior Design and Typesetting: Kristi Smith, Juicebox Designs

Printed in the United States of America
12 13 14 15 16 17 RRD 8 7 6 5 4 3 2 1

To my mom

Chapter One

YOU'D THINK THAT meeting Jesus face to face, as I did six years back, would give you a leg up in the Christian life.

I'm still not sure why Jesus chose me to dine with him one night at Milano's Italian restaurant in Cincinnati. Maybe God knew that my resistance to him was a mile wide and an inch deep. I was thirty-three, outwardly successful, with a beautiful wife and two-year-old daughter. Behind the veneer, our marriage was in shambles, I doubted myself as a parent, and I wondered where in the world anyone could find the secret to life.

I received an anonymous invitation to dine with Jesus. Surely a prank by the guys at work. So I showed them. I arrived at Milano's and sat down to eat my free meal—across from a guy who claimed to be Jesus. Only thing, it actually *was* Jesus, patiently answering my questions, waiting for me to set aside my relentless skepticism and open my heart to the reality of a God who loved me and who died and rose to save me.

The encounter transformed my life. In the span of one evening I traversed the chasm between cynical agnosticism and faith in God. Three weeks later my wife, Mattie, had a similar encounter with Jesus on an airplane. Except Jesus didn't identify himself to her. He just let her figure it out.

Ever since those encounters we've been followers of Jesus.

For two years afterward, life was great. How could it not be? I had met Jesus. He had explained everything. Well, not everything, but a lot of things. Life made sense. It had a purpose. I was full of joy, peace, and all that.

But I slowly lost it, whatever "it" was. My closeness to God, my excitement about Jesus, the sense of purpose and meaning he brought. I'm not sure when it started fading. I hadn't lost my faith. Far from it. But the life that faith was supposed to produce—where was it? I thought meeting Jesus would energize me for a lifetime. But for the past four years I had been slowly coasting downhill.

The distressing thing was, I'd been doing all the "right" things to be a good Christian. After our Jesus encounters, Mattie and I decided to join a church. Wasn't that what Christians did? Naïve as we were, we chose the closest one: a nice, mid-sized suburban church. The preacher talked too long (a quarter of the people had their eyes closed and I'm pretty sure they weren't praying) and the worship band played songs that didn't exactly make me feel worshipful. Admittedly, meeting Jesus himself may have jaded me; I constantly found myself thinking things like, "Jesus wouldn't go for this song."

Fortunately, the church had plenty to offer besides Sunday services. Mattie and I joined a home group. If any place offered an authentic experience of Jesus—beyond what we had already experienced, of course—it would be a small group dedicated to that purpose. After all, that's what the twelve disciples were, a small group experiencing Jesus together.

Our first evening there, the leader invited us to tell the group a little about ourselves. I was happy to oblige.

"I became a Christian five weeks ago when I had dinner with Jesus at Milano's. Mattie sat next to Jesus three weeks later on a flight to Tucson." I turned toward her. "You two even ran into each other during a layover in Dallas, didn't you?"

"At Starbucks," Mattie chimed in. "It was the weirdest thing, this guy sitting next to me on these flights. Have ... have any of you ..." Her speech slowed. "Actually met Jesus ... like that?" Apparently not. The group stared at us as if we were from another planet.

We found a new church, vowing never to mention our Jesus encounters again—not to Christians, at least.

Our second church was smaller, a bit more diverse. We joined another home group and, through our silence, felt welcomed. Unfortunately, this group seemed more intent on addressing "felt needs" than on actually experiencing Jesus. One night, after watching our second video series on parenting (following a series on marriage and family finances), I remarked to Mattie, "If people were walking closely with God, wouldn't some of these issues take care of themselves?"

I joined a men's discipleship group, but I encountered the same problem I felt everywhere: I didn't fit in. Men in the group were consistently sharing opinions about God that contradicted what I had personally experienced with Jesus at Milano's. When I said things like, "I know Jesus wouldn't see things that way," they looked at me like I was nuts. Who was this guy, a new Christian, to presume to know what Jesus would and wouldn't think?

The last straw for me was an exchange with the group leader. He was teaching about John 15, Jesus' message on the vine and the branches.

"The key to living the Christian life is abiding in Christ," he declared.

"And how do we do that?" I asked. Jesus must have forgotten those instructions in our time at the restaurant, because I didn't have a clue. I was always the one asking, "What does that mean exactly?" when it came to spiritual platitudes that, I discovered, were tossed around churches like beanbags at a school carnival.

"We abide by keeping Jesus' commandments," he responded.

I pondered that assertion. "So you're saying that to live the way we should, we abide, and to abide, we have to live the way we should."

The leader smiled patronizingly. "It's just one of the mysteries of the faith."

It wasn't a mystery of the faith at all; it was circular reasoning.

I left the men's group, redoubling my efforts to draw near to God on my own. After meeting Jesus, spending time with God had been easy. I knew he was right there with me, just as Jesus had been at our dinner. I could sense him speaking to me directly from the Bible.

After a time, however, that sense disappeared. God seemed distant. I got distracted by life. Paying the mortgage and attending kids' events took precedence over being alone with God.

How could I reconnect with him? Through the Bible and prayer, I figured. But the Bible didn't encourage me anymore. Instead, it screamed at me from every page: YOU AREN'T MEASURING UP! GET YOUR ACT TOGETHER! WHY AREN'T YOU A BETTER CHRISTIAN?!

And my prayers? They just bounced off the ceiling right back at me. I wasn't communicating back and forth with Someone; I was just mouthing syllables. My times with God felt hollow. I didn't feel like praising or thanking, to say nothing of confessing or supplicating.

Nor did I feel like doing any of the other things I was supposed to do as a Christian, like witnessing or going on mission trips. What was I supposed to tell people about the abundant life Jesus offered? I hadn't found it myself! I wasn't loving enough toward my wife, patient enough with my kids, or trusting enough about the future. The worst part was knowing I'd actually regressed. Not long before, I really had been laying down my life for Mattie, patient with the kids, trusting God, and telling people about Jesus. I had been excited about him. What happened?

The bottom line was, I was no longer living the kind of Christian life I wanted to, and I didn't have a clue what to do about it. I had followed all the spiritual formulas and I had gotten nowhere.

I was stuck.

Life events didn't help my frame of mind. After two miscarriages, Mattie was six months pregnant with our third child. We'd been nervous about trying again, but at six months at least we were starting to breathe easier. This pregnancy was going as planned.

I was excited about having another child, but my enthusiasm was tempered by my spiritual state. I had so wanted to pass along a vibrant, living faith to my kids. I had actually met Jesus! What an advantage my kids had spiritually! But Sara, eight, was now old enough to witness how little clue I had about what it meant to walk with God.

Jacob, three, would see it himself one day. Was I bringing another child into the world only to witness his father's spiritual charade? Our church was already full of couples whose kids had failed to see the reality of Christ in their parents' lives and had walked away from the faith. I was afraid our children would soon become a similar statistic.

All of this came crashing upon me as I drove past downtown Chicago, heading south. I'd traveled this route many times. In daylight, I would look admiringly at the skyline set against the majesty of Lake Michigan. This time, it wasn't the lack of sunlight that kept me staring at the road. It was the dimness in my soul.

Where is God in the midst of all this? Why doesn't he answer my prayers for help? Am I doomed to a life of mediocre Christianity? I have everything going for me, but I feel empty on the inside. It seems like I'm just stumbling around in the darkness, without so much as a flashlight to give me direction.

My despair shouldn't have surprised me. I had just left my folks' house on Chicago's north side. Spending time with my folks—especially my dad—always made my thoughts spiral downward, even when our visit was cordial. This one wasn't.

I had only agreed to go to Chicago under considerable duress: the logic of Mattie.

"Nick, it's your parents. They want to give us furniture as they downsize. We should take it."

She'd walked to the kitchen table, sat across from me, and smiled that impish smile I never could resist. "We could all go—make it a four-day weekend to Chicago and back."

I rolled my eyes. "Are you crazy? Four days with my dad? I'm already down on myself enough these days. I don't need Dad adding to that."

"Nick, you're just . . . struggling. We all do."

Right. Mattie was the only person I knew who didn't seem to struggle with her spiritual life. It all came so naturally to her.

"Besides," she continued, "your dad's not so judgmental anymore. He's mellowed."

"Being around him still makes me feel like I did as a kid. I never can measure up."

I finally relented. I flew up on Friday and rented a U-Haul Saturday morning. Dad helped me load the furniture for my Sunday morning ride back to Cincinnati. The first twenty-eight hours there, all went smoothly.

In the twenty-ninth, Dad blurted out one of his infamous queries.

"When are you finally going to get a real job, Nick?"

We were watching a Cubs game. He didn't take his eyes off his HDTV.

"Dad, I have a real job. I'm a consultant." I could feel the tension crawl up my neck.

"Uh-huh." He reached for a tortilla chip and dipped it in some salsa. "Where's your office?"

"My clients don't care that I office out of the house. I go to their workplaces."

He was silent for a few moments. Alfonso Soriano hit a double. Dad didn't blink. "So how's business since the recession?"

I shook my head. He wouldn't give up. "It's taken a while to pick back up."

He leaned forward slowly and extracted another chip from the bowl. "I figured. Income's down too, I bet. Are you two making it?"

I turned to him. "Yes, Dad, we're making it fine." My tone was curt. I knew he could tell I was getting annoyed.

"Uh-huh." He dipped his chip and ate it. "I'll tell you who really is doing fine."

Oh, brother. Here it came. Comparing me to my sister, Ellen, an attorney for the Environmental Protection Agency in DC.

"Who?" I asked, as if on cue.

"Ellen."

What a shock.

"Just got a promotion, you know."

"No." I stared at the game.

"And set financially. Did you know she has a guaranteed pension? By the way, how have your 401k's done the last few years?"

I could feel the vein in my neck throbbing. "They tanked in the downturn. I already told you that."

"Yeah, and you sold low." He reached for the beer on the end table and took a sip. "Mattie and the kids are counting on you providing some security, Nick. Especially with another one on the way. If I were you, son—"

I rose from my chair, seething. "You aren't me, Dad, and I'm not you. If you were me, you'd still be working at Pruitt."

"It was a good job for you, son."

"Right. And they were falsifying environmental data for client reports. That's a federal crime."

He turned back to the TV and watched another pitch, ignoring me while I stood in the middle of the living room. He finally reached for another chip. "It just seems to me that Mattie would be happier if you were a little more . . . stable."

"No, Dad—you'd be happier." I strode toward the kitchen, then turned abruptly, my voice rising. "And I am stable. I've only had two jobs in nine years. That's stable."

I reached for my keys and wallet on the kitchen counter just as my mother emerged from their bedroom.

"What's all this yelling?"

I forced my face to soften. I wasn't mad at her, although she never did stick up for me when Dad was putting me down. "Dad thinks what I do for a living isn't good enough."

"I didn't say not good enough!" The reply came from the living room. "I said too unstable. Plus your investments—"

"That's enough!" I shouted. I stomped down the hall to my bedroom, threw my stuff in my bag, and walked back to the kitchen.

"Bye, Mom. Thanks for the furniture." I kissed her perfunctorily on the cheek.

"You're leaving?"

"Yes."

"But Nick, it's nine o'clock. You can't drive home at night."

"Sure I can. Did it in college all the time." I walked to the side door to avoid the living room. "I'll call you next week."

She glanced nervously toward the living room. "Aren't you going to say goodbye to your dad? And thank him for helping you load up?"

"I said thanks earlier." I opened the door and stepped out, then turned back to her. "If he wants to apologize for anything, he can call me."

I closed the door, climbed in the U-Haul, and drove away, leaving my dad behind. What I couldn't leave behind was the effect he had on me. I was forty years old, for goodness sake. Why did it matter what he thought of my life? But it did. It always did.

I felt doubly bad because of the way I had reacted. My dad knew exactly how to press my buttons and get me to overreact. And when I did, all of my Christian veneer vanished. I was the same old Nick blowing up at my dad like I always did. It was never his fault, of course. He never lost his temper. Just asked questions. Innocent questions.

Ever since I'd met Jesus, my dad believed I was just going through a religious phase. It would blow over. Or (worse, from my perspective) it wouldn't change anything about me.

Getting mad, stomping out after nine o'clock at night—I could just see my dad walking into the kitchen, getting another beer, and saying to my mother, "He must have left his religion in Cincinnati again."

Butting heads with my dad filled me with both anger and guilt. Heading south, I looked in my right side mirror and saw the lights of Chicago fading behind me. Despite the beauty of the city, I felt empty every time I drove away from this place.

My next move didn't help matters. I picked up my cell phone and called Mattie to tell her I was on my way home. I gave her the short version of what had happened at my folks'.

"You did what?"

"I walked out. Look, Mattie, I don't need you getting on my case too. My dad is bad enough."

"I am not getting on your case, Nick." She sounded stern with me. "I just think you're going to have to apologize to your parents."

"Me apologize? Are you kidding? My dad is the one who needs to say he's sorry. He's been treating me this way my whole life. And now you're standing up for him."

There was silence on the other end. "Are you finished?" she finally said.

"Yes."

"Then I'll see you when you get home. I'll pray that God keeps you awake. Bye."

"Bye."

Great. Now everyone was mad at me.

I needed a distraction. I turned on the radio and slowly scanned the AM dial, landing on a health talk show. Someone called in about low testosterone. *Maybe that's what I need, more testosterone. I could use a boost.* I listened to the host's response. *Okay, maybe that's not what I need.*

Someone called in about toe fungus. My mind wandered. I scanned highway signs and billboards and caught myself starting to play the alphabet game, a family favorite that Sara always seemed to win.

I wallowed in my funk through Gary, onto Interstate 65, and past Merrillville. I glanced down at the U-Haul's fuel gauge. Almost an eighth of a tank. I didn't feel like stopping yet. *This gas tank is huge. Rensselaer is only twenty miles. There's a station there.* I drove on.

I knew I was in trouble when my engine started sputtering ten minutes later. I pressed on the gas pedal. *Kerplunk. Kerplunk.* I glanced at the fuel gauge. *One-sixteenth of a tank. Can't anyone make an accurate fuel gauge anymore!*

I pumped the accelerator. Nothing. The truck slowed. I glanced in my side-view mirror. Darkness. I was stuck in the pitch black in the middle of nowhere. Somehow, it seemed fitting. When the truck slowed down to thirty, I pulled over to the shoulder and coasted. I glanced at the clock. 11:27. And only a month ago I let our AAA membership expire. *Brilliant move, genius.* I glanced in my side-view mirror again. One pair of head-lights. *Not many cars to wave down. Not that I'd want to. But there's no way I'm going to ask Mattie to drive two hundred miles to bring me a gas can.*

Fortunately, I had a savior: my Blackberry. Surely I could find a twenty-four-hour tow service to run me some diesel. And charge me an arm and a leg. Between this and paying for the U-Haul, I could have bought new furniture.

The truck rolled along the shoulder and finally came to a stop. I sat and stared out past the front of the truck.

There, my headlights illuminated a man holding a fuel can.

It was Jesus.

Chapter Two

AT THE SIGHT of him, I spent several seconds in shock. I had wanted to get back together with Jesus ever since we'd had dinner. That hope had faded with time. I never expected to see him again. In this life, I mean.

Once I got over the shock, other emotions started flooding in. Anger, for one. Why had it taken him so long to reappear? Why had he left me hanging out to dry for six years, leaving me on my own to make the Christian life work?

And guilt. My behavior at my folks' hadn't exactly been a model of Christlikeness. More like a cauldron of resentment and unforgiveness.

But along with the guilt and anger, I felt a glimmer of hope. Perhaps now I would finally get the answers I had been looking for.

I reached for the door handle, but Jesus had already started walking toward my side of the truck. I rolled down the window. He smiled and held up the can. "Need some diesel?"

He looked the same as he had before: average height, short dark hair. Wearing jeans and a light blue denim shirt, he appeared less imposing than he had at the restaurant.

"You just happened to be standing here in the middle of nowhere with a gas can?"

"It didn't take a prophet to tell you weren't going to make it to the next station. These things don't even get ten miles a gallon, you know."

"I know."

I got out of the truck and removed the gas cap. He pulled out the spigot and poured the fuel in. After a few moments, he spun the cap closed and sealed the can. "That'll get you to a truck stop about five miles down."

"So, you're just out here helping stranded motorists?"

"I thought you might enjoy some company. Have room for one more?"

I shrugged my shoulders. My lingering anger kept me from acting too excited about his appearance. "Sure. I will in a minute."

I opened the passenger door and removed a rocking horse from the seat and two boxes from the floor. "It's all yours."

I put the items in the back of the truck and glanced at the furniture to see if anything had shifted during the ride. Everything looked okay. *Not that I'd care much if something got scratched.*

We got in the cab. I glanced at Jesus. "You changed out of your business suit, I see."

"Jeans seemed appropriate."

An eighteen-wheeler zoomed past us. I looked in my side mirror. The interstate was empty save for a pair of headlights far behind us. I accelerated on the shoulder and pulled onto the highway.

"This cab isn't the best place for a deep conversation. Pretty noisy." I looked over at him. "We could have met at a restaurant again."

He shook his head. "This is the right place and time."

"Have you been planning this meeting a long time, like you did the last one?"

"Let's just say I knew you'd need another one."

"And are you going to meet with Mattie again too?"

"No, Mattie's doing fine."

By implication, that meant I wasn't. Maybe I would be if Jesus had bothered to reappear a little sooner.

We rode in silence for a few moments. I had stashed so many questions away in the intervening years, I didn't know where to start. And now that Jesus was actually sitting next to me, I could hardly remember any of them anyway. I couldn't get past the irritation I was feeling. I decided to start with that.

"So." I didn't turn toward him. "Where exactly have you been the last six years?"

"I've been where I always am."

"I thought we were getting together for more dinners."

"Who said that?"

"You did. You know—the card you gave me with the Bible verse on it? Revelation 3:20? 'If you open the door, I will come in and dine with you.'"

"Yes?"

"Well, we haven't done any more dining."

"You haven't spent any time dining with me since then?"

"You mean, like, devotional times? Reading the Bible and praying?"

"That's one way."

"Sure." I finally glanced his way. Our eyes met. "But lately it seems like I'm the only one at the table."

"Maybe that's something we need to talk about."

"Maybe you should have talked to me about that at our first dinner." My words had an edge to them.

The truck stop appeared on the left. I exited, pulled up beside a diesel pump, and got out. Jesus stayed in the cab.

I felt bad about the way the conversation had started. Sure, I was mad at God. Things hadn't gone like I thought they would since meeting Jesus. But the truth was, I was glad to see him. Our first encounter was the opportunity of a lifetime. Now he was giving me another. How could I be bitter?

I finished pumping and got back in the truck. I started to turn the key, then sat back. "Look, I'm sorry for being angry. I suppose . . . I suppose you already knew I was."

He gave a slight nod.

"I'm just frustrated with my Christian life, and I can't seem to get answers. But here you are. That's timely, I guess."

The corners of his mouth turned up. "I'm glad to be here too, Nick. In the flesh, that is."

I fired up the engine and we got back on the interstate. I felt self-conscious about the quality of the ride.

Here was God the Son sitting in my U-Haul, bouncing up and down on a stiff seat. He didn't seem to mind.

Jesus looked around the cab. "Do you have anything to eat?"

I glanced at him in surprise. "You came hungry? There's an apple in a sack on the floor, plus a box of Cheez-Its."

"Thanks."

"Sorry about the crumbs on the seat."

He bent down and got the apple. We rode silently while he ate. The longer we sat, the more uncomfortable I felt. Here was the one person in all the universe who knew me inside and out. He knew the good, but what pressed down upon me was the awful reality that he also knew the bad. I could hide what I was like on the inside from everyone else, even Mattie to a certain extent. But not Jesus. And that was making me squirm.

I finally couldn't take it anymore. "Okay, go ahead and say it."

He took another bite of his apple. "Say what?"

"You know. What you're thinking."

"Which is?"

I glanced toward him. "What a failure I've been. How disappointed you are in me. How I should have been living differently the last six years. Well, four at least. And tonight, how I should have reacted differently at my folks' house."

"What makes you believe that's what I'm thinking?"

"Because it's the truth, isn't it? After all, you know everything. I can't hide anything from you."

He reached down and placed the apple core in the paper bag. "Nick, it sounds as if you're the one who's disappointed."

He'd hit the nail on the head. "Yeah, that's a good summary. I am disappointed. I'm disappointed in the whole Christian life. It just doesn't work for me. The abundant life you promised—who were you kidding? Or was that meant for just some people? Because despite everything I've tried, I'm just not experiencing it."

There it was, out on the table. I'd been told so many times, "Be honest with God." Praying by myself, there never seemed much point in telling God what he already knew. With Jesus sitting next to me again, however, honesty seemed like the best route, though I immediately felt guilty for expressing my bitterness.

"So what's not working for you?" Jesus asked.

"You already know."

"I want to hear it from you."

I sighed. "Okay. Everything. Spiritually, I mean. Things were easy after Mattie and I met you. We read the Bible and prayed together. We talked about you all the time. I actually had a sense that God was meeting with us. We joined a church. We started doing family devotions with our daughter Sara. She was excited about God, even at age three. She used to dance around the house singing 'Holy, Holy, Holy.'"

Jesus chuckled. "She had good taste in hymns."

"I started serving on the outreach committee at our church. I got involved in the men's program; I was meeting with three other guys in a discipleship group. I went through the leadership training class."

"And then?"

"Somewhere in the midst of it all I lost contact with God. After you and I met, fellowship with God was great. But after a couple of years it started to feel burdensome, like a duty I had to fulfill. I hate to say this, but the Bible became tedious. I studied it because I was supposed to."

I gathered my thoughts, unsure as to whether I wanted to plunge ahead. *But he already knows all this. There's no point in not admitting it.* "I've gotten to the point where point where my prayers just seem to bounce off the ceiling. I can't remember the last time God answered one. Not that I would have noticed, probably. I don't like going to church. I don't encounter God there. I'm tired of pretending to be something I'm not. I never tell anyone about you anymore. What am I supposed to say? 'Come to Jesus! Be miserable like me!'"

He laughed. I couldn't help a slight snicker myself. It sounded ridiculous, but that's the way I felt.

An eighteen-wheeler had been gaining on us. It got too close for comfort, changed lanes, and passed. I shot him a dirty look. Normally I would have sworn at him, but with Jesus in the truck . . .

"If you're tired of pretending to be something you're not," Jesus asked, "what exactly do you think you should be?"

"A good Christian."

"And how would you define that?"

"Someone who actually does what the Bible—what you—tell us to do. Someone who isn't impatient with his wife and kids, who isn't resentful every time he has to do something inconvenient, who actually cares about people rather than avoiding being around them, who shows God to people in a positive way, and leads people to Je—, to you."

I glanced in my mirror again. "Who doesn't swear at drivers on the road."

"You didn't swear at that semi driver."

"Yeah, but I would have if you weren't here!" I exclaimed, exasperated. I rolled down my window to get a little fresh air. The road noise was too great to have a conversation. I rolled the window back up.

"What bothers you the most?" he asked. "That you aren't behaving like a Christian should behave, or that you aren't as close to God as you were, or even closer?"

"Both," I admitted. "When you boil it down, those are the two main things. I'm tired of being a hypocrite. And I'm tired of feeling so distant from God. I just don't know how to get close to him—to you—anymore. I do love God. I mean, I guess I do. The whole thing just seems so burdensome."

He shook his head. "That's the second time you've used that word."

"I can't even listen to Christian music anymore. This abundant life and unending joy they sing about—I don't know anyone who experiences that. Well, Mattie, maybe. I wish I could go back to listening to my old secular CDs."

"Who's stopping you?"

"I trashed them all. I went to a Christian conference that convinced me everything from Metallica to REM to Simon and Garfunkel's greatest hits was satanic. So— wanting to obey God, and be holy for him—I got rid of all my non-Christian music. The great CD purge of 2006."

"That's too bad. Simon and Garfunkel had some good stuff. You could download them, you know."

I looked over at him. *How weird was this? Jesus talking about downloading music? Not something he ever discussed on the hills of Galilee.*

A pair of headlights passed us going the opposite direction. I looked in the rearview mirror. No other traffic was in sight. We were completely alone.

"I suppose what really annoys me is Mattie." I took a deep breath. This was going to sound petty. "I resent where Mattie is spiritually."

"Which is where?"

"Far ahead of me."

"Why do you say that?"

"The way she relates to God. He's so real to her. She's always seeing deeper things in the Bible. The way she acts toward the kids—she's so much better with them than I am. And I hate to admit it, but she's a better wife than I am a husband. That bit about laying down my life for her like you laid down your life for the church—that's a total joke. I try to be loving, but then I revert to my old selfishness. I mean, she has her faults too . . ."

There wasn't any point in listing Mattie's shortcomings. I didn't think that would go over real big with Jesus.

"We met you within weeks of each other, and now it seems like she's light years ahead of me. And I don't know how to catch up."

"I wasn't aware it was a race."

"You know what I mean. Maybe I just haven't been committed enough. But to be honest, I'm tired of it all. What's the point of having another quiet time, or listening to another sermon, or attending another home group meeting? It's not going to change anything." I looked over at him. "I'm sorry. I tend to get pretty discouraged when I'm out of fellowship with God."

"Out of fellowship?" He looked surprised. "How did that happen?"

"Well, you know. I wasn't exactly the most loving son around my parents tonight. Then I snapped at Mattie on the phone. And my bad attitude . . . I just haven't taken the time to confess any of it and get back into fellowship."

Jesus glanced out his window. "Stop the truck."

We went under an overpass. I looked at him. "What? What is it?"

"Stop the truck! Pull over. Now!"

I pulled the truck onto the shoulder and slowed down. "Why? What's wrong?"

"I have to get out."

"What for?" I was starting to feel alarmed.

The truck came to a stop. Jesus unbuckled his seat belt and reached for the door handle. "I can't be in here with you." He got out and closed the door.

I unbuckled myself, leaned across the seat, and rolled down the window. "Why not?" I was thoroughly baffled by his behavior.

He took a step back from the truck. "Because we're out of fellowship."

Chapter Three

"WHA—WHAT DO you mean?" My words sounded shrill.

He folded his arms across his chest. "You have un-confessed sin, so we're out of fellowship, and we can't be back in fellowship until you confess and get forgiven. Isn't that what you said?"

"Yes, but . . ." He was right, but somehow that didn't seem to apply if he was with me in the flesh. "We were already talking in the truck."

His eyebrows rose. "Oh. Well, in that case . . ." He uncrossed his arms and took a step toward me. "So you're saying it's okay for us to talk even if we're out of fellowship?"

I leaned back into my own seat and sat straight up. "I . . . I'm not quite sure."

He stood on the side step and put his elbows on the sill. "Your theology is really messed up, you know that?"

"I'm just saying what they teach us."

"Nick, there are realities in the spiritual realm that you haven't even thought of accounting for. Let me tell you one: you and I are never out of fellowship."

Never out of fellowship? That made no sense. "But what about when I sin?"

He shook his head. "Fellowship simply means sharing something with someone. You know what we share? My life. When you trusted in me, I came to live in you. I became one with your spirit. Permanently. That's as close as someone can get. When you sin, that connection isn't broken. It can never be broken. You can't be connected to me one minute, separated the next. You're always connected."

"But don't I need to be forgiven for my sins?"

He sighed and shook his head. "What do you think happened at the cross?"

"You died for my sins."

"Yes. So all of your sins are forgiven."

"But don't I still need to get right with God?"

He leaned his head through the window. "Nick,

all your sins are forgiven. Period. Past. Present. Future. They're all gone."

"But . . . I don't need to confess them?"

"I didn't say you don't need to agree with Spirit when he points something out to you. I said your sins are already forgiven and we're never separated. Just agree with the Spirit and thank him that it's already forgiven." He crossed his arms again and glanced up and down the highway. "Now, should I get back in the truck, or do you still think we're out of fellowship? It's a little chilly out here."

I smiled. "Please, get back in."

"Great." He opened the door and hopped in. "I didn't want to have to walk."

I started the truck again and pulled onto the interstate. Half a mile down we passed a car on the shoulder with its parking lights blinking and the hood up. I glanced at it in my mirror. "Shouldn't we go back and help them?"

"No."

I looked over at Jesus. "But aren't we supposed to help someone like that? If you see your brother in need . . . all that stuff?"

"He called OnStar."

We passed a mileage sign. Indianapolis 78. Cincinnati was two hours beyond that. I had three hours to get the answers I wanted—assuming Jesus stayed with me the whole way.

"So don't you have any advice on all of this?"

"Your spiritual struggles?"

I nodded. "Any input?"

"It sounds like we have some work to do in your life, doesn't it?"

I sighed. "Yeah, it does."

"Maybe we should come up with a plan."

That sounded hopeful. I'd always been a plan kind of guy. As a management consultant, my work consisted of developing strategic plans that others then implemented. Jesus knew my language.

"Great," I answered. "Where shall we start?"

Jesus shifted toward me in his seat. "Let's start at the top. How about your devotional times? How have those been going?"

I knew he would start with that. "Not very well. I used to have a regular quiet time with God. I'd get up early, spend some time in the Bible, have a time of praise, then have really meaningful times of prayer. But now . . ."

"It sounds like we need to get back to that sort of routine. Daily. How much time would you like to aim for?"

I was tempted to say an hour—that seemed like an appropriate amount of time to give God. Realistically, I got bored after twenty minutes. I compromised. "How about forty minutes, first thing in the morning."

He nodded. "Sounds good. Before the kids get up?"

"Definitely." Swinging by the gym before work already made me pressed for time most mornings, but I'd managed it before, I could do it again. I did some mental calculations. "I'll need to get up at 5:20. Is there a prayer pattern you recommend?"

He waved me off. "Let's get the structure down and then go back and fill in the details. So that's your devotional time. What about a separate Bible reading plan?"

I knew that simple Bible reading was the key to any good Bible study program. "Not much the last year or two, unfortunately. I got a read-in-a-year Bible, but I haven't used it. Yet." It was only supposed to take twenty minutes a day.

"Great. Why don't you dive into that. What about Scripture memory?"

"I used to do three verses a week, plus review."

"What if you tried memorizing large passages instead of isolated verses? You could probably do twice as many verses a week."

That was a great idea. I'd thought once about memorizing the whole Sermon on the Mount. "That sounds good. Hey, could you write this stuff down? There's a pen in the glove compartment."

"Sure, glad to." He retrieved the pen and jotted some notes on the back of my rental contract. "Okay, now what about concentrated Bible study?"

I sighed. "Well, I can rejoin my men's group. I wasn't always thrilled with it, but it did get me deeper into the Word."

"How long did it take?"

"To do the homework? Thirty minutes a day, to do it decently."

"When's the best time for that?"

"At night, I guess, after the kids go to sleep. There's no other time slot."

We passed a truck stop. I glanced down at my gas gauge. Still above three-fourths of a tank. I wasn't going to make the same mistake again.

Jesus jotted down some more notes. "All right, what about church attendance?"

That was one area where I hadn't fallen off, miraculously. "We go every Sunday, both to the worship service and the Sunday morning classes. We could go Wednesday night, I guess."

"But your men's group meets every Friday morning, doesn't it?"

I nodded.

"That seems like enough," he commented. "Okay, speaking of the men's group, is that a place where you get real accountability? Where other men can keep you on the straight and narrow in every aspect of your life?"

I shook my head. "We don't really share at that level. There's a discipleship program at the church where they do that. You're assigned a discipler."

"How often would you meet with him?"

"Once a week, I think. Plus accountability calls throughout the week."

"Okay." He wrote again. "Now, you really need to be giving and not just receiving. Are there any guys you could disciple?"

Discipling someone was the last thing I felt qualified to do. "A while back I was thinking about getting involved with a couple of the college guys. Maybe I could lead a

Bible study in our house. Surely I'm farther along than some of them."

He smiled. "Surely. So when could you do that?"

"Some weeknight. Thursday, maybe."

"Super. Speaking of giving, how's your evangelism going?"

My shoulders slumped. "I feel like a total failure on that front."

"When was the last time you led someone to me?"

"Three years ago, maybe more, back when Mattie and I were inviting neighborhood friends over for dinner to share the gospel."

"How often could you do that?" Jesus asked.

"We could do it every"—I thought better of over-committing—"how about once a month?"

"Great. Now, how about your family's spiritual life?"

We covered family devotions: I'd start with fifteen-minute daily devotions with the kids. Missions: We'd do a short-term overseas mission trip at least every other year. Reading material: I'd start reading good Christian books again, maybe thirty minutes a night. Spiritual leadership in the home: I'd initiate devotional times for Mattie and myself, fifteen minutes a day. Then we got to financial giving.

"We were tithing 10 percent until a couple of years back, but then Mattie had some medical bills, and I started cutting back on our giving, and we haven't got back to that level."

"Ten percent to the church or to everything?" Jesus asked.

"Everything. Are you saying we should give 10 percent to the church, and then more to other organizations?"

He shrugged. "You might want to think that through. Was your 10 percent pre-tax or post-tax?"

"Post-tax." I glanced at him. "Are you saying we should tithe pre-tax?"

"Well, that's a heart issue, isn't it?"

Man. Ten percent pre-tax. That was steep. I did a quick mental calculation. Since Mattie and I were both self-employed, our marginal tax rate was over 50 percent. If we had to tithe on our pre-tax total income, that would be almost 20 percent of our take-home pay. And that was only to the church. If we gave to other causes . . . how could we possibly afford that?

I wrenched my mind back to our conversation. Before we reached the city of Lafayette we'd covered time management, organizational skills, budgeting and financial discipline, submission to authority, quality marriage time, and use of entertainment.

"All right," Jesus finally said. "That's probably enough for now. There are some categories we haven't addressed, of course."

"Like what?" It seemed like we'd been fairly thorough.

"We don't have to cover it all right now."

That was fine with me; we had covered enough. But I had to admit I was feeling pretty good about getting Jesus' personal input on a spiritual plan. Especially in his own handwriting.

He folded the paper he had been jotting notes on and handed it to me. I turned on the overhead light and glanced down the sheet. It wasn't the safest thing to do, but I figured Jesus wasn't going to let us get into an accident.

I did some quick mental math. Personal quiet time, forty minutes. Kids' devotionals, fifteen minutes. Devotional time with Mattie, fifteen minutes. Bible reading, twenty minutes. Bible study, at least thirty minutes. Christian reading, thirty minutes. Over two and a half hours. And that didn't include men's group meetings, discipleship meetings, accountability calls, meeting with college guys, evangelism dinners, more quality time with Mattie, or Scripture memory.

We rode silently as I let it all sink in. Over three hours a day added to a schedule that already seemed way too busy.

I finally turned to Jesus. "This program isn't going to work, is it?"

He looked at me, his eyes meeting mine. "Nick, when I was here on earth, do you think I lived by a program?"

Chapter Four

HALF AN HOUR outside Indianapolis, we passed the last thing I wanted to see: a large, brightly lit billboard.

EROS ADULT VIDEO
"Stop and indulge your fantasies"
24 HOURS
EXIT 130, 6 MILES

I glanced over at Jesus. He was looking straight ahead. *Maybe he didn't see it. If we can just get through the night without discussing this topic.*

I decided to return to where our conversation had left off. "Are you saying I shouldn't do any of the things we listed?"

"As a means to an end, some of them are fine. But you've got the cart before the horse. You want to know what's really wrong with that plan?"

"Yeah."

"What's wrong is that its starting point is always you. Here's what you have to do to get your act together. Here's what you have to do to get spiritual. But that doesn't work. The starting point for this life isn't you. It's me."

Well, of course. How many times had I heard it before: it's all about Jesus. "Fine, but how do I make that work?"

He shook his head. "You don't make it work. That's the whole point. Do you want to know why things have always 'worked' spiritually for Mattie, and why it doesn't seem like they have for you?"

That was precisely what I wanted to know. "Yes, I would."

"Two years after we met, you started treating me like a task to fulfill. Do this checklist. Do this program. Then you've accomplished your spiritual homework."

"But that's mostly what they do at our church."

He nodded. "I know. But it doesn't work, because it's all about you. Mattie, on the other hand, has never forgotten that she and I are about relationship. She doesn't have a program. She has a person she stays closely connected to. For her, it's all about me."

"But I tried to stay close to you!" I couldn't hide my frustration. "I just didn't know how. There was no one to teach me."

"That's why the Holy Spirit lives in you."

I started to respond, but he raised his hand and cut me off. "But . . . since I'm here now, maybe I can help a bit."

A road sign came into view. Exit 130 was next. As we neared it, Jesus leaned forward and said, "Turn off here."

I looked over at him. "Here?"

"Yes, here."

I took the exit ramp. The access road led to a stop sign at an overpass. Across the highway was a large truck stop. *Maybe he needs a bathroom break.* Somehow, that didn't seem quite right.

"Straight or turn?" I asked.

"Straight."

Straight? I went through the intersection. The adult video store was several hundred yards ahead on the right. We approached it.

"Take a right in here."

"Into the video store?"

He nodded.

"You want to go into a porn shop?"

He smiled at me. "I want you to turn in here, please."

I turned in, feeling utterly uncomfortable with the situation. I stopped the truck on the left side of an eighteen-wheeler, sixty or so feet from the entrance. We sat for a few moments, facing the entrance. A man came out of the store, glanced at us, and walked the other way across the parking lot.

Another guy came out. He was in his fifties, wearing jeans and a long-sleeve denim shirt. He headed toward the truck next to ours, walking quickly and averting his eyes. As he walked between our trucks, Jesus rolled down his window. Without looking at us again, the man placed his foot on the step to his cab.

Jesus' voice almost caused me to jump out of my seat. "You're joined to God, aren't you?"

The man paused a moment, then without turning, opened his cab door.

"You're joined to God, aren't you?" Jesus repeated.

The man pivoted and looked at Jesus suspiciously. "Yeah, I guess you could say that. Wouldn't know it by my being here, would you? How'd you know?"

"I know these things. Say, we're going back to the truck stop for some pie and coffee."

We are?

"Would you like to join us?"

From anyone else, the invitation would have sounded . . . well, gay. Who invited a stranger at a porn shop for coffee?

The man glanced at me, then locked his eyes on Jesus. His face softened a bit. "Most guys don't come here looking for midnight conversation."

"Sometimes God doesn't give you what you expect."

"What are you, a pastor or something?"

"Sort of. I have a flock."

The man glanced away toward the truck stop, then back at us. "Why not? It's not like it can get much more embarrassing than this."

"We'll meet you there."

Jesus rolled up his window and turned to me. "Ready?"

"Ready for what?"

"Pie and coffee."

We drove back to the truck stop, which had a twenty-four-hour restaurant inside. Jesus and I sat down in opposite sides of a booth for four. The trucker from the parking lot joined us a minute later, sitting next to me. We made introductions all around. His name was Larry.

"Call me Jay," Jesus said to him. It was the oddest social situation I had ever encountered, but Jesus seemed entirely comfortable with it.

A dour-looking waitress walked over and poured us coffee. "What'll it be for you gents?" she said as if she had asked the question a thousand times.

We took a moment to look over the menu. Jesus spoke first. "I'd like a slice of blueberry pie, Betty."

I glanced at the woman's nametag.

"One blueberry," she confirmed. "A la mode?"

"Which way do you like it?" Jesus asked her.

"Honey, I don't eat 'em, I just carry 'em."

Jesus chuckled. "Then let's make it plain."

"One plain blueberry."

She turned to Larry and me. We both opted for the coconut cream. "Two coconuts," she repeated. "I'll have those right out."

We sipped our coffee, then Larry broke the silence. "I have no idea why I'm here. I guess it was just crazy enough to feel right. Plus my haul isn't due into Nashville until in the morning."

"What are you carrying?" I thought a little small talk seemed safe enough.

"Furniture," he replied. "Furniture parts, actually. To some manufacturer."

"Really?" I responded. "I'm carrying furniture too." I looked at Larry and realized the comparison was a bit overblown. He was driving a commercial eighteen-wheeler; I was driving a twelve-foot moving van. "Not quite the same, I know. My furniture is from my folks."

"Did they pass away?"

"Oh, no. Just moving into a smaller place."

The waitress arrived with our pie. Jesus said "thank you" for all of us; Betty disappeared behind the counter again.

I was having my first bite when Larry changed the subject. "So, you two—what are you, some sort of intervention team?"

I looked at Jesus, who grinned at me. He turned to Larry. "I've done some interventions."

"Did my wife send you?"

Jesus smiled and shook his head. "No, definitely not."

Unlike Jesus' approach with me six years before, it didn't appear he was going to reveal his identity to Larry just yet. Maybe he knew Larry wouldn't believe him, just as I hadn't at first.

Larry looked at me. "And what's your story?"

"I, uh . . ." If Jesus wasn't going to reveal his identity, I certainly wasn't about to. But how was I supposed to explain why I was here with Jesus? "I ran out of gas on the interstate. Jay here was . . . Jay stopped and helped me out."

"So this is the first time you've met?"

Jesus and I looked at each other. He didn't jump in with an answer.

"No," I responded. "We met six years ago."

"Really? Wow. What a coincidence. Where'd you meet? At church?"

"Uh, no. At a restaurant in Cincinnati. That's where I live."

"Well, it feels a little weird running into fellow believers in the parking lot of a porn store."

"Not as strange as you may think," Jesus replied. "You've done it before, I'm sure. You just didn't know it."

He looked at Jesus. "Yeah, probably so. Kind of pathetic, isn't it?" He had a bite of his coconut cream pie. "Well, if you're here to try to cure me of some kind of pornography addiction, forget it. I've tried it all."

"Actually, we're just here to hang out." Jesus turned to me. "Larry might be interested in some of your story, Nick—how you went from being an atheist to a believer in Christ; what life's been like since."

Oh, great. How am I going to pull this off without talking about literally meeting Jesus? "Well, as I said, I met Jesus six years ago."

Larry corrected me. "You said you met Jay here six years ago."

I glanced at Jesus, who wore a slight grin. *He is actually enjoying watching me squirm!*

"Right," I answered. "It happened about the same time." I gave him a bit of background, talking about my family, growing up in Chicago, my dad taking me to Cubs games.

"Cubs games?" Larry rolled his eyes. "You know, I was liking you fairly well until you said that." He smiled, reached behind him, and pulled a baseball cap out of his back pocket and placed it on his head. A Chicago White Sox cap.

"So you've suffered almost as much as I have."

"Hey, we won the Series in '05 in four games. When was the last time the Cubs—"

I held up my hand. "I know. The Roosevelt administration. Teddy's. It's rooting for the team that counts."

He shook his head and chuckled. "Okay, go on with your story. At least now you have my sympathy."

The cross-town ribbing didn't bother me; I had dished it out and taken it for almost forty years. I continued my story: my marriage to Mattie, our children, my hostility to Christianity. "But then I met Jesus—"

"How did that happen if you were so antagonistic to God?"

"God revealed himself to me in a personal way. I just knew Christ was real."

"And what's it been like since then?"

I sighed. There didn't seem to be any escape from my spiritual struggles of the past several years. I gave him the abbreviated version. He nodded frequently during my story, as if he had experienced a good deal of it himself.

"You know," I finally admitted, "I can relate to your struggle with sexual sin."

His eyebrows rose. "You're caught up in pornography too?"

"At this point, no. But I used it before I got married. And I used to sleep around a lot." I glanced at Jesus, knowing that statement was a bit misleading. "Well, after I got married too."

"Sleeping around? After you got married?"

"No, not sleeping around. Pornography. It only stopped when I met Jesus he—" I resisted the impulse to nod Jesus' way, or to finish saying *here*. "When I met Jesus," I simply repeated.

Larry shook his head. "I wish mine had stopped then. And you haven't been tempted since?"

I glanced down at my wedding ring. "I wish. This last year I've been tempted more than I'd like—especially on business trips. The hotels all have it. My last trip, I glanced at the adult video options until I saw how much they cost."

"At least you stopped."

"Only because I'm cheap." I looked at Jesus. "I can't seem to resist looking at women way longer than I should, whether in person or just passing magazine racks." I glanced around to see if anyone was within earshot, but the place was virtually empty. A lone trucker sat across the restaurant having some coffee. I could hear someone else playing a video game across the room, several aisles of merchandise away. "After I became a Christian. I thought the lust issue was gone for good, but . . ."

"Same with me." Larry shook his head. "I've struggled with it since I was a teenager. Then I became a Christian in my twenties, and the habit went away, but within a year I was back looking at magazines and going to adult movies. That was back when they actually had theaters. Pretty seedy."

"Did you try to stop?" I asked.

"Of course. I tried everything I knew. I changed my route to work to avoid going past one theater. I cancelled my *Sports Illustrated* subscription because of the swimsuit issue. Once videos came along, I got a VCR, then I got rid of it after I started renting adult videos. Then I cancelled my cable. Then I got rid of my TV."

"None of that worked, I assume."

"No. I just had to work harder to get the porn. I got rid of my ATM card and stopped carrying cash so I wouldn't have money for it. I stopped driving my car and rode the bus to work, which was a major pain. I even cancelled my newspaper because of the lingerie ads."

"That's pretty extreme."

"It didn't work, either."

I thought about Larry's efforts, none of which helped. "Pardon me for saying so, but it seems like those were all logistical things. Did you try any spiritual solutions? Pornography seems like a spiritual problem to me."

"Oh, sure. I tried a slew of spiritual things. I memorized all the scriptures on lust and fighting sin. I meditated on Scripture. I made a list of all the ways porn was hurting me and my witness and reviewed it every day. I put on all the Ephesians 6 spiritual armor every day. I started going to a charismatic church and had the pastor cast out the demons of lust and pornography."

He leaned back in his seat. "I tried an accountability group. I even called one of the guys in the group hourly for a couple of days, just to check in. That didn't stop me. I committed myself to reading only Scripture. I went on a mission trip to Russia, hoping that would jump-start me spiritually. I ended up sneaking out of the hotel and buying porn on the street in between our evangelistic outreaches."

I laughed at that one. "Sorry," I said. "I know it's not funny."

"No, I understand. It's pretty insane." He had another bite of pie. "I did do one thing that seemed to work for a while."

"What was that?"

"I got in a support group that met at a church. That helped some. But then the Internet came along, and we moved to another town, and I fell back into it all over again."

He drank some coffee and shook his head. "I know this is killing my relationship with my wife. And with God. There's got to be a way out, right? I mean, if God can't deliver you from this, what does that say about Christianity? But I haven't figured out the answer yet. I guess I've kind of stopped fighting it."

He turned to Jesus. "You've been awfully quiet, sitting there. Have you ever struggled with lust?"

"I've been tempted," Jesus answered.

It sounded strange to hear him say that, but that's what the Bible said, so I shouldn't have been surprised. I figured Larry would ask him more—I would have—but he seemed too caught up in his own dilemma.

"Maybe," Larry said, "this is just the way it'll be until I get to heaven. I used to think God had provided for victory over this kind of thing . . ." He looked at me, then focused his attention on Jesus. "If you've only been tempted, then you must have found the secret. What do you have to say about this?"

Jesus sipped his coffee and leaned forward. "I say you guys have no idea what happened to you in the realm of spirit the moment you believed."

Chapter Five

"ANYTHING ELSE I can get you gentlemen?"

I was so focused on what Jesus had just said that I hadn't noticed Betty approach the table. She poured Jesus and Larry more coffee. As she leaned across the table to pour mine, she winced in pain.

"Stiff neck?" Jesus asked.

She looked at him and nodded. "Guy rear-ended our pickup. I called the chiropractor, but he's on vacation."

Jesus slid out of his seat. "Maybe I can help." He pointed to her neck. "May I?"

"What are you, a physical therapist?"

"I dabble a bit."

She looked at me, shrugged, then slowly turned around. He reached up and pressed his thumbs into the back of her neck and held them there. Betty tensed, then relaxed. "Wha—" Her face broke into a smile as she bent her neck from side to side. "The pain's gone." She turned to Jesus. "What did you do?"

He smiled at her. "Just a little something I know. Say, we're stepping outside for a few minutes. Can you hold our booth?"

"Sure, hon." She gathered our empty pie plates with a bit more zest than before. "You have to be fifty feet from the entrance to smoke, though. State ordinance."

Jesus looked at me, grinned, and led the three of us out the door. He looked around as if to make sure no one else was out there, then walked over to the U-Haul and leaned against the hood. We followed.

"What do you think happened the day you put your faith in Jesus?" he asked.

It was a little weird hearing Jesus refer to himself in the third person. Was he not going to tell Larry who he was? It was all I could do not to spill the beans every time I opened my mouth.

"We got forgiven," Larry answered.

"And what else?"

"We were declared righteous," I offered.

"And what else?"

We were silent for a moment, then Larry spoke. "The Holy Spirit started the process of changing us to be like Christ." He looked at me, then back at Jesus. "Well, theoretically, at least."

Jesus shook his head. "A lot more happened than that. Do you want me to show you?"

"Show us?" I asked.

Jesus straightened, took a step toward me, and reached out his hands toward my eyes. I resisted the impulse to step back. I closed my eyelids as his hands touched them. I opened them just as he was placing his hands on Larry's eyes. I was surprised Larry let him do that. I didn't have time to dwell on it, though. An awareness suddenly encroached upon my consciousness. My vision had begun to change.

I didn't realize it at first, because I still could see the physical objects around me. But I was also seeing more. A faint aura appeared around Larry's head, as if he were glowing. My eyes were drawn irresistibly to the center of his being. From his core emanated a bright glow of pure white light. Surrounding the source of the light was a brighter, even purer light. It encompassed the first light and circled around it and wove through it in such a way that the two lights at one moment looked distinct, the next moment merged. Yet there was no sense of time passing between the two states; the lights were simultaneously merged yet retained their distinctiveness.

I was hypnotized by the effect, by the light's purity and beauty. For a period of time—I don't know how long—I couldn't draw my eyes away.

Finally I became aware of another, similar glow radiating nearby. I took my eyes off Larry and looked around. I could now see the source of the other radiance.

It was me.

From the center of my being came the same lights, one brilliantly pure, the other even more so, the two sources somehow joined as one.

For some time I was aware only of the reality of the lights within me. The enormity of the revelation overwhelmed me. At some point I regained a sense of physical presence, and my gaze returned to Jesus standing next to me. I looked at him for a moment before saying anything.

"These lights—they are the Holy Spirit?"

"One of them is."

"And the other?"

"The other is your human spirit. That's what the Holy Spirit gave birth to inside you the moment you believed." He turned to Larry. "And inside you, when you believed."

Larry looked into me, then into himself again. "How are we seeing this?"

"I opened your eyes to the spiritual realm," Jesus answered. "Part of it, at least."

"I'm not seeing you this way," Larry said.

Jesus nodded. "In time. Right now, I would be too bright for you."

"What are you, an angel?"

Jesus smiled. "No, but the Father did send me."

I became aware of movement to my left. I turned and glanced at the entrance to the truck stop. What I saw felt like a punch to the stomach. A man had stepped outside the door. In his core, where Larry and I had the two bright lights, was a darkness so loathsome, a void so gruesome that the mere sight of it filled me with an indescribable sense of emptiness.

"Oh!" I grimaced as I turned away. "Oh . . .!"

I looked at Larry, who held onto the sight a moment longer before wrenching his eyes away. I heard the man's footsteps across the pavement, followed by the opening and closing of a cab door. I wanted to look toward him again, but I couldn't. The engine started, the gears shifted, and the truck drove off.

My eyes met Jesus'. "What was that?"

"That," he said, "is the human spirit you two once had—before you were born from above."

Chapter Six

FIVE MINUTES LATER, sitting in the restaurant booth, our sight had returned to the mere physical realm, but my mind was still trying to comprehend what we had seen in the spiritual realm. I could only imagine what was going through Larry's head. He had no idea who he had been talking with, which I'm sure was why he still looked completely stunned.

I had a million questions, but I stayed silent, letting Larry regain his bearings. Finally he looked at Jesus and spoke quietly. "What are those other heavenly beings called? Seraphim? Cherubim?"

Jesus nodded.

"Is that what you are?"

"No. But I'm from the same place, you might say."

Larry looked at me, incredulity still in his eyes. "But you—you seem like me."

I nodded. "That's because I am. I'm just a guy."

"But . . ." He seemed to be sorting through the whole night's experience. "You said you two had met before. So this person . . . " he nodded toward Jesus, "this person is for real?"

I smiled. "Oh, yes, very real."

"And he is really from God?"

"Definitely. Meeting him . . . well, it's how I came to faith in Christ. Whatever he shows you, you can trust."

Larry looked back over at Jesus and stared at him a moment. "I believe you," he said, seemingly to me. "I don't know why, but I do."

I turned to Jesus. "The spirit we saw of the other man—you're saying that's what used to be inside us?"

He nodded. "That's what's in everyone before the Spirit births a new human spirit in you. It's a human spirit dead to God, without his life."

Larry leaned forward and spoke quietly again. "And the light we saw in us—you're saying the Holy Spirit actually gave birth to that?"

"Of course," Jesus replied. "'That which is born of the flesh is flesh; and that which is born of the Spirit is spirit.' What did you think Jesus meant when he said that?"

Larry shrugged. "I never really thought about it."

"Which, in part, is why you're having the problems you're having. You don't understand the change that occurred in you. You're still thinking of yourself as a sinner at heart, as someone for whom it's natural to sin."

"But that's what I've always been taught," Larry objected.

"Then you have to decide what to believe—what God says, or what religious tradition says."

I was still thinking about the dark spirit. "So what happened to our old spirit?"

"God removed it, just like he promised he would. Ezekiel 36."

I looked at Larry, then back at Jesus. "You'll have to refresh us."

"'I will give you a new heart and put a new spirit within you; and I will remove the heart of stone from your flesh and give you a heart of flesh. And I will put My Spirit within you . . .'"

Larry ran his hand through his hair. He had the look of someone who had just won the lottery and was still letting it sink in. "So you're saying God actually did that—took our old spirit out and put a new one in?"

"Yes. That's what he said he would do."

"What did he do with our old spirit?" I asked.

"He crucified it on the cross with Jesus. Romans 6:6. Haven't you two ever read this stuff?"

Romans 6. That's a Bible chapter I actually did know fairly well. Our old man was crucified with him, it said. "But I thought that was just positional truth."

Jesus leaned back and put his arm on the booth seat behind him. "Positional truth. I'm not sure what that means. Maybe you can enlighten me."

Uh-oh. I wasn't prepared for a theological debate with Jesus. "It means . . . well, it means that's the way God looks at things . . . because . . . I am in Christ? Isn't that what it means?"

He shook his head. "God sees things as they actually are, not as he pretends they are. We're talking actual reality here, not some heavenly accounting system that God keeps glancing at to make sure you're on the right side of the ledger. The old spirit you saw is real. The new spirit in you isn't positional. It's real. It was birthed by the Holy Spirit. It is like Jesus is, holy and righteous. And when God says he took your old man—the inner being you were before—and crucified it on the cross, trust me, that event was real."

I glanced at Larry. He looked confused. "But Jesus died two thousand years ago," he said. "I put my faith in Jesus twenty-three years ago. How could my old spirit . . ."

"Be placed on the cross?"

"Right."

Jesus leaned forward. "Because unlike the physical realm, the spiritual realm isn't time-based. Things in the spiritual realm simply are, without regard to time. That's why Jesus is the Lamb crucified before the foundation of the world. That's why you were chosen before the foundation of the world. That's why your sins were all forgiven, even before you had committed one. Your old spirit was placed on the cross, judged, and executed with Jesus. That's why there can't be any condemnation. There's nothing left to condemn. The old you is gone. You have a new spirit, created in Jesus' image. God sees you as righteous because he has made you that way in your deepest being. Just like you two saw a few minutes ago."

I glanced over Jesus' shoulder. Betty was approaching with a pot of coffee. She stopped at the booth next to us and gave a customer a refill, then came to our table. "You gents don't seem to be in a hurry to get anywhere."

She filled each of our cups. I pulled out my Blackberry to check the time. 2:11. I was fine, for now. I just needed to get to the house before Mattie got up and started worrying about me.

"How's your time?" I asked Larry.

"Are you kidding? I wouldn't leave now for nothing." He turned to Jesus. "So I don't get it. If we've been given a new spirit, born from God, why do we still sin? Shouldn't we be sinless?"

Jesus smiled. "One day. Sin, as a force, has been re-moved from your inmost being, that's true. That's why Paul says that you died to sin. Sin has been cut off from your inner man. Your problem is that sin still dwells in your body, which unlike your spirit, hasn't been remade yet."

"Our body? But it seems like it starts in my thoughts."

He nodded. "It does. But you're forgetting that the brain is part of the body. Your whole body, including your brain, has been programmed from birth—before that, actually—to sin, to live independently from God, trying to make life work on its own. That's flesh. It will be that way until you get a new body."

I let out a sigh. "That's not particularly good news. You seem to be saying that even our new spirit isn't enough to overcome our body's programming."

Jesus emptied a pack of sugar into his coffee and stirred it. "It's not. But it was never meant to. Remember what wars against the flesh?"

"The Spirit," I answered.

"Right. The Holy Spirit. Only the Spirit can overcome the flesh in you. 'Walk by the Spirit, and you will not carry out the desire of the flesh.' It was never God's plan for you to overcome by yourself, even with a new human spirit."

"So what's our new human spirit for, if it can't overcome the flesh?" Larry asked. I was wondering the same thing.

Jesus leaned back in his seat and sipped his coffee. "It does two things. First, it gives you the want to. Now, deep down, you want to obey God, even if you keep failing. Before, with your old spirit, that wasn't true. You were a rebel at heart. Second, your new spirit makes it possible for the Holy Spirit to join himself to you—to make you one with God, permanently."

"Because he wasn't going to join himself to the old spirit that we saw earlier," I interjected.

"Correct," said Jesus. "He wasn't going to make himself one with that. Only with the new spirit he birthed. That's the whole point of everything God did—providing you forgiveness, giving you new birth, everything."

"For the Holy Spirit to dwell in us?" I asked.

"For the Spirit to join you to the Trinity. The Father, the Son, and the Spirit are all one. Now you are one with them. They are in you, to live their life through you. That was always their plan, to make humans an expression of their very own life. You"—he looked pointedly at each of us—"you two are that expression."

Larry looked at me and shrugged. "You sure wouldn't know it by how I've lived."

Jesus' eyes were filled with compassion as he turned to Larry. "That's because you've never understood that you're not the one who lives the life. It's Jesus' life. Only he can live it."

"And what do I do?" Larry asked.

"Simple. You trust him to do it."

The man in the adjoining booth rose, pulled out his

wallet, and put some cash on the table. He was sixty, perhaps, wiry, strong, wearing a cowboy hat and boots.

"Didn't mean to eavesdrop, but I couldn't hep hearin' a bit of what you men were sayin'." He took a toothpick out of his mouth and continued. "I don't know much 'bout the Spirit, but I do know God gave us his rules in his instruction manual. We jus' need to keep 'em." He tipped his hat to us. "Drive safe, podners."

"Drive safe," Larry responded.

"You too," I added.

Jesus remained silent. The man walked out the door.

"Why didn't you say anything to him?" I asked Jesus.

He smiled. "Didn't need to. He's right where the Father has him." He glanced at the man outside getting into his truck. "But he was wrong about something."

"Not knowing much about the Spirit?"

"No, about keeping God's rules."

"What's wrong with what he said?"

"Just one thing. There are no rules."

Chapter Seven

LARRY AND I looked at each other, then back at Jesus.

"What do you mean, there are no rules?" I asked.

He leaned back and folded his hands behind his neck. "*Rules* is just another word for *law*. You died to the law with Jesus. You were released from the law. Jesus is the end of the law as a means of living rightly. How many different ways does the New Testament have to say it?"

Larry jumped in. "But how can there be no rules? God didn't do away with the Ten Commandments. "

"No, not for everyone. Just for you."

"For me?"

"For all believers. The law had one purpose: to show you your sinfulness, to show your need for a Savior. Once you come to faith in Christ, it's done its job. After that, trying to live by the law—by your own efforts to keep it—doesn't produce abundant life. It produces spiritual death. Isn't that what you've been experiencing?"

Larry sighed. "Yeah."

Jesus turned to me. "And you?"

"Yeah."

"Do you want to know why?"

We both nodded.

"Because your new inner man longs to obey God. You want to reflect him. So you see the commands, and you try as best you can to obey them, and that puts you right back into self-effort, which doesn't work. It never works."

"God never meant it to work." The excitement had returned to Larry's voice. A look of realization had crossed his face. "My flesh can't reflect him, can it?"

A pleased laugh seemed to hide behind Jesus' smile. "No. It can't. It never will."

"Deep down, I want to obey God," Larry continued, "and I try to, but I can't."

"Romans 7," I mused.

"But . . ." Larry nodded, as if to himself. "Jesus in me can."

Jesus leaned forward. "And he will. He's doing it

now, and he will do it more and more as you train your inner eye to see one thing."

"Which is what?" I asked.

"'It is no longer I who live, but Christ lives in me.'"

We sat in silence for a moment. "But what about the New Testament commands?" I finally asked.

Jesus grinned. "You just can't let that go, can you?" He pushed his coffee back. "Your new heart—the one you saw tonight—wants to obey, Nick, and that's a wonderful thing. The other wonderful thing is that the Obedient One lives in you. He will take those commands and make them promises. He will fulfill those in you more than you ever dreamed."

Jesus turned and motioned to Betty, who walked over.

"Do you have a check for us, Betty?"

Betty reached into her pocket, tore off a bill from her pad, and handed it to him.

Jesus looked up at her. "Thanks. You've been wonderful."

She smiled. "Thank you, Jay." She walked toward the counter.

"We're leaving?" I asked. "Now?"

"I think it's time for Larry to hit the road."

Larry glanced at his watch. "I don't mind being a little late to Nashville."

Jesus shook his head. "No, that's enough for tonight."

All of a sudden, I feared that not only was our time at the restaurant over, but my time with Jesus might be over too. "But you just told us the secret to the Christian life. Aren't you going to explain more?"

He rose from the booth and put his hand on my shoulder. "There is no secret, Nick. Not like you mean. There's just a Person. He's the secret." He left a generous tip on the table and walked to the cash register. I watched him chat with Betty. I had the same thought I'd had at the restaurant six years before: *he genuinely likes being around people.* I wished I could always say the same.

I looked back at Larry. "Well, I guess that's it."

He shrugged. "If it is, that's okay, I feel like a new man. I am a new man, I guess. I can't wait to get home and tell my wife. If I told her on the phone, she'd never believe me." He shook his head. "I'm not sure if she'll believe me even in person."

I knew that feeling.

Jesus returned from the register. "Ready?"

We walked out and angled toward our trucks, stopping first at Larry's. Larry shuffled his feet for a minute, then looked at Jesus. "This has been incredible—the most incredible thing that's ever happened to me."

"You know what? The Father thought the same thing the day you joined his family."

Larry seemed stunned by the statement. "Thanks," he finally said. He reached into his pocket, pulled out his keys, and glanced at his truck, then back at Jesus. "Jay, will God send someone to me again?"

Jesus reached out and put his hand on Larry's shoulder. "He already has, Larry. The Holy Spirit will teach you everything you need to know. You just need to ask him— and learn to listen."

Larry stepped forward and they embraced. "Thanks," he repeated. He opened the door to his cab, climbed in, and rolled down the window. "I feel like I could live off this night forever."

Jesus smiled. "Well, you will live forever. As for the other, Jesus will be there when you come down off your high."

Larry nodded. "I know."

We said our goodbyes. Larry started the truck and

pulled out of the parking lot. We walked to the U-Haul. I breathed a sigh of relief when Jesus climbed in the passenger side.

"You're traveling on with me?"

He strapped on his seat belt. "We're not done yet."

I pulled out of the parking lot, drove down the access road, and got on the interstate. It was just past 2:30; traffic was still sparse.

"Why didn't you tell Larry who you are?"

"That wasn't best for him."

"But it was for me six years ago?"

"Everyone gets what they need."

"Even if they don't deserve it?" I asked, somewhat rhetorically.

"Deserving isn't the issue. The Father never blesses people based on how good they've been. He blesses based on his love and his purposes."

I glanced in my side-view mirror and saw headlights in the distance. Traffic would start to pick up as we approached Indianapolis, even at this time of night. But for the moment, we had the road to ourselves. It felt like the late night drives I took with buddies during college. We always thought our conversations got so deep, which in retrospect seems laughable. But there is something about driving late at night that causes people to open up and discuss the more serious side of life.

"What will happen to Larry?" I asked.

"He'll live off tonight's high for a while, then he'll settle into a spiritual routine by turning what he learned tonight into a formula."

"A plan?"

"Not exactly. More like a how-to. That's the trap almost everyone falls into. Do this and you'll be a successful Christian. Believe this and you have it made. In Larry's case, trust in what God accomplished at the new birth, and at the cross, and trust me to live my life through him. That'll be his formula for a while."

I was confused. "But I got the impression that we do need to believe those things."

He nodded. "Yes, they're important. Believing truth is vital. But it's not the secret."

"Larry left thinking it was." So did I.

"That's true. And he'll end up where most believers end up—frustrated and without enough answers. Then he'll be ready for the answer."

"I thought there wasn't a secret."

"There's only one, if you want to call it that."

"And that is . . .?"

"Me." I looked over at him and our eyes met. "I'm the life, remember? Everything I accomplished at the cross was for this purpose: to join you to me, that I might live in you. It wasn't to get you forgiven. It wasn't to get you right with me. It wasn't to crucify your old man. It wasn't to give you a new man. But all those things had to be done to accomplish my goal: making you one with me—eternally. That was the only way I could share my life with you and express my life through you."

"But how does that translate into how I live my life? You're not going to do the whole thing for me."

"No, it's a joint venture. But your emphasis has been far too much on yourself, far too little on me. You remember that verse I quoted from Ezekiel?"

"Sure. God will take out the old heart and give me a new one."

"The verse goes on. The Father says, 'I will cause you to walk in my statutes.' 'Statutes' is Old Covenant talk, of course. You're no longer under any law but the law of love. But the point is this: I'll cause you to walk in love. Because it's me in you living my life, which is love."

"But doesn't that destroy free will?"

He smiled. "No, never. As I said, it's a joint venture. I live the life. But you must choose to cooperate."

"And how do I do that?"

"By trusting. By making yourself available—completely abandoned to me. By stepping out and being the hands and feet of love as the Spirit leads you. I'm living the life, I'm the source of the life, but it will always look like you. Just as it always looked like me when the Father was living his life through me. That's all that was happening when I was here on earth. I couldn't do anything on my own. He was living through me."

"But that was easy," I objected. "You were God."

"True, but I had to operate as fully human, as humans were intended to operate: joined to God, with his life flowing through them. I had to do that if I was going to be your substitute. I'll tell you a little secret, though, as to how I always remained in the Father—always abided in Him."

"How?"

"By knowing that I was perfectly loved."

"But . . ." I watched as a car passed us on the left. "But you're God's only Son. Of course he loves you that way."

He replied gently. "Nick, you have to know some-thing—something you've missed ever since we met. The Father loves you exactly as he loves me. You must know, in the depths of your being, how deeply you are loved."

I drove silently for a few moments. Finally I said, in a quiet voice, "I don't know how to do that."

He nodded. "I know you don't. We'll give you a glimpse."

Chapter Eight

WE DROVE AROUND Indianapolis on 465 and hit Interstate 74 toward Cincinnati. Whatever Jesus planned to show me, he wasn't in a hurry.

Twenty miles south of 465, he glanced up at a road sign. "Get off at the next exit, would you?"

I looked at the sign. Shelbyville. *Why would Jesus want to get off at Shelbyville, Indiana?* I exited on Highway 9, took a right as he directed, and drove a mile to the town. We turned right on a downtown roundabout and exited onto Washington Street. Two blocks later, Jesus said, "Pull in here."

Major Hospital.

I stopped the U-Haul in the parking lot and turned to Jesus. "You're not going to go and heal a bunch of people, are you?"

He laughed. "No. Not tonight."

"So what are we doing?"

"We're going in."

He opened his door and slid out. I joined him behind the truck. "Are we here to see someone in particular?"

"Yes."

"Anyone I know?"

"No."

I followed Jesus through the main doors and to an elevator bay. We rode to the third floor and walked into an area labeled "Labor and Delivery."

"We're going to see a baby? At this hour? But aren't there rules about visitors . . ."

"Trust me, Nick. We're going to see a family." He pointed to a waiting area. "Why don't you hang out over there a minute."

I ambled over and took a seat, watching him as he approached a nurses' station. In a moment he and a nurse disappeared around a corner. I was tempted to follow, but Jesus had told me to wait. I leaned forward and grabbed a parenting magazine off the coffee table in front of me. I started reading an article titled "Adding Number Three." Timely.

The author had almost convinced me that having a third child was virtually effortless when Jesus returned with another nurse, who was beaming. Had he told her who he was?

"You ready?" he asked me.

"For what?"

"To go see the family."

"I guess."

"This is Emily." He motioned toward the nurse, then toward me. "Nick."

She reached out her hand and we shook. "So very glad to meet you," she effervesced.

I followed them past a security door into the nursery. We stopped in the hallway and looked through the viewing window into a large room with incubators. Premature infants lay in two of them. A third infant was being rocked by a man—evidently the father—in street clothes wearing a surgical mask. His eyes were fixed on the baby, who was connected to at least three machines by tubes and was asleep.

"It's so small," I commented. I had held two babies in my arms so far. Thankfully, both had been full-term and perfectly healthy. I couldn't imagine holding one so small that it virtually fit in the palm of your hand, or one hanging onto life by a thread. Who could endure that?

"Some are smaller than that," Emily remarked. "Down to two pounds—that's at twenty-eight weeks, usually. Earlier than that, we have to transfer them."

Twenty-eight weeks. Mattie was in her twenty-sixth.

The nurse glanced at Jesus. "I'll let you two watch her for a few minutes. I'll be at the station at the end of the hall."

She walked down the hall. I looked back at the baby, then at Jesus. "So do you know this family?"

"Not personally. Not yet. But I wanted to show you this."

I looked back at the father and child. "Show me what?"

"The best illustration on earth of what our love for you is like."

I looked more intently at the scene in the rocking chair. The father was gently stroking the infant's hair, a look of peaceful delight adorning his face.

"This is the closest most humans ever get to mirroring God's love," Jesus said. "Most human love is performance-based. Do well enough, act right enough, please the other person enough, and you'll be loved. If not, you'll be rejected. I know your dad's love was like that, Nick." I turned to Jesus and he looked into my eyes. "And I know you still bear the scars of that. But it was the best he could do. It was all he knew from his dad, having to measure up to be accepted, to be loved. He never felt good enough. That's all he had to pass on."

I could feel the beginnings of tears wanting to well up in my eyes. I pushed them back. Crying in front of Jesus was the last thing I wanted to do. But hearing him acknowledge the pain I had carried for so long—*why can't my dad love me the way I am?*—just hearing that brought a measure of peace. Jesus knew. He understood.

He looked back at the father and child. "That baby can't do anything to earn her father's love. She can't even nurse yet. All she can do is gurgle and poop. But she is deeply loved, simply because she exists. She is loved unconditionally—no performance required."

The father inside glanced up and looked around. His eyes met mine and he smiled. After a moment, they returned to the face of his child.

Jesus turned to me. "That's the Father's face toward you, Nick."

I looked at Jesus. "But what about when I blow it? I've blown it pretty bad at times."

He nodded. "I know. But you know what effect that has on our love for you?"

I shook my head.

"None. Nothing you do can make us love you less. And nothing you do can make us love you more. That's because our love isn't based on what you do; it's based on who we are. We are love." He turned to look inside the nursery again. "When was the last time you went to the ocean?"

Living in Cincinnati, we didn't pop over to the beach too often. "We went to Virginia when Mattie was pregnant with Jacob. That was four summers ago."

"And did you go swimming in it?"

"Sure."

"How much wet did the ocean have?"

"How much wet did it have? The whole thing was wet—it was the ocean."

"Exactly." He looked at me. "Nick, we are like the ocean. The ocean doesn't have wet—it is wet. You jump in, you get wet. God doesn't have love—we are love. Our love isn't a possession. We can't give it away as a reward to those good enough to earn it. Love is simply who we are. We love you because of who we are. You were created to be the object of our love, to share in our love. Nothing you do can change that.

"God is love. That hasn't penetrated the depths of your being. God is love. If God simply had love, we could love you today and withhold our love tomorrow. But no, God is love. That's our nature. Loving you is as natural to us as breathing is to you. We never stop loving you. Everything we do toward you, we do in love. Our love is like the air around you, which you live in and can't escape. The air constantly presses down upon you. Our love is that way. It presses down upon you. Endlessly. Infinitely."

"But I don't feel loved by God."

"I know. That's why you struggle so much. That's why Larry struggles so much, why he keeps visiting porn shops. You're trying desperately to fill the hole in your heart, all the while thinking that if you perform well enough, we will finally love you. But here's the truth: you won't function properly in any area of life unless you know in your deepest being that you are unconditionally, limitlessly loved by us."

"But I don't know how to experience your love." And I wanted so much to be able to experience it.

He nodded. "You will."

Motion in the nursery caught my attention. A nurse had entered and was talking with the father. He smiled, rose from the rocking chair with the baby, and walked over to the incubator. He paused and I could see his lips moving close to the baby's ear. He kissed her gently on the forehead and placed her inside her incubator.

He followed the nurse out to the hallway where we were standing and removed his surgical mask. His eyes were moist. He stood there looking a bit lost.

"What's your baby's name?" I asked, knowing full well that I was simply uncomfortable with the silence.

He gave me a slight smile. "Avery."

"How old is she?"

"Four days. She, um . . . she's having respiratory problems. But they're optimistic." He nodded toward the nurses' station.

Jesus stepped forward. "Avery will be fine. She has a wonderful family."

The father sighed, then looked Jesus in the eye. He didn't look away, but stared at him for several moments. He finally nodded. "Thank you. I know she will be."

He stepped past us and walked down the hall.

Avery will be fine. When Jesus said someone would be fine, they would be fine. I was glad for the father, and I was glad to have witnessed his love for his baby. For the moment, it did make me feel more connected to God's love.

I just didn't know how it could translate into feeling that way most of the time.

Chapter Nine

TEN MINUTES LATER, we were walking across the parking lot to the U-Haul. Jesus had spent several minutes talking alone with the nurse at her station before we left.

"Did you tell her who you were?"

"I didn't have to. She knew."

"You'd met her before, like with me?"

We went around to our respective sides of the truck and got in.

"No, never as with you."

I started the engine. "Then how did she know who you were?"

He shrugged. "She knows me well—very well."

We drove out of the parking lot, out of Shelbyville, and back onto the interstate. Within a couple of miles we hit some highway construction. The lanes narrowed and the inside shoulder disappeared, replaced by cement barricades.

"So our conversation back there about God's love . . ." I glanced in my side-view mirror. The traffic on the interstate seemed to be picking up. A few more eighteen-wheelers were rolling, at least.

"Yes?"

"Are you saying sin doesn't matter?"

"Not as far as God's love, it doesn't."

"But doesn't God have to punish sin?"

He sighed. "This really is a difficult concept for you, isn't it? What do think the Father did at the cross? Your sin was placed on me. I actually became sin. The Father poured out his wrath on me." He unbuttoned his sleeves, folded down the cuffs, and held up his hands in the air, displaying the nail prints in his wrists. I had seen them once before. I couldn't help staring at them again.

He continued. "Don't you believe what I did was sufficient? Nick, the sin issue is done. Compared to God's love, your sin is like throwing a pebble against Hoover Dam. It doesn't affect it in any way."

"I know," I responded. "It just feels like—"

He shook his head. "It doesn't matter what it feels like. I'm describing what is. We love you because of who we are, not what you do or don't do."

"But what about God's discipline?"

"Our discipline is training, not punishment. Everything we do toward you now is out of love, not punishment. I took the punishment. If we discipline you, it's to train you so you can be more like us. Why do you think you are here, anyway?"

"On earth?"

He nodded.

I thought about that for a moment. "I always assumed it was to serve you."

He shook his head. "Do you really think we need your help? You weren't created to serve us. That does end up happening, because we're family. But you were created to be loved, to be a part of the love the three of us have always had for one another. That's your significance—you are brought into the very heart of the Godhead, to be one with us. That's the highest you can possibly go. You're already there. And now, you're in the first steps of living that journey."

"It feels like I've been stepping backwards."

"Sometimes you have to take a step back before you plunge ahead. It's not a detour; it's part of the process. You've been trying to make life work in a way that's impossible."

I was trying to focus on the conversation and my driving at the same time. I wasn't used to maneuvering a U-Haul through such narrow lanes.

"How have I been doing that?" I asked.

"By not truly knowing you are loved by God. Newborns are like toys—batteries aren't included. But toys have to have batteries to operate as designed. For people, the battery is God's love. Without personally knowing how deeply you're loved, without living in our love, you can't function. Not as you were designed to. Being filled with God's love means being filled with God himself. And someone who overflows with God will bear all the fruit God ever intended—love, joy, peace, patience, kindness. Sound familiar?"

"The fruit of the Spirit."

"Exactly. We produce it through you when you are filled with our love. You become an expression of our love. It has nothing to do with keeping rules or trying as hard as you can. It's about being filled with us. Everything we allow in your life, we allow for that purpose: being filled with us, and expressing us."

I was about to ask another question when my cell phone rang. I glanced at the clock. 4:15. It had to be Mattie. I felt around on the seat next to me and finally located it.

"Nick, I'm bleeding." She sounded panicked and as if she had been crying.

"Vaginal bleeding? When? For how long?"

"I don't know. I got up to go to the bathroom and felt it. Nick, I'm scared."

"It's all right." I could already feel my blood pressure rising, my body tensing to leap into action. I glanced at Jesus, but I couldn't read him.

"You just need to get to the hospital," I said to her.

"Carol is coming from next door to stay with the kids and Jim is taking me to Good Samaritan."

"Mattie, I'm just past Shelbyville. I'll meet you at the hospital."

"Okay." There was a pause at her end. "There's Jim. I need to go."

"Okay, I love you."

The connection ended. I reached up to the dashboard to put my cell phone in a more accessible place, but there was no flat spot there. I turned on the overhead light and looked around the seat. The U-Haul had no console . . .

The blaring of an eighteen-wheeler's horn jerked me upright. I had drifted into an on-ramp lane and was inches away from the merging truck. I wrenched the steering wheel to the left and veered across two lanes of interstate. I yanked it back to the right to straighten the U-Haul, but I was too late. Before I had fully straightened, I heard metal scraping against the cement construction barriers.

Glaring lights appeared in my right side mirror. Another eighteen-wheeler swerved past me, its horn blasting. I glanced at my mirror but saw no other trucks. I slowed and edged away from the barriers, my heart pumping for all it was worth. I pulled over to the outside shoulder and slowed to a stop, letting out a deep breath as my head collapsed into my arms against the steering wheel.

"That was close," I mumbled into my sleeve. *But why had Jesus even allowed it? He could have warned me.* I lifted my head up and started to open my mouth. My lips fell back together. He was gone.

Chapter Ten

I LEANED BACK into the seat and stared blankly ahead. The last time we'd been together, Jesus and I had shared a nice, leisurely parting. We hugged. He gave me a verse to look up. He promised that he would dine with me.

This time, nothing. No promises. No words of encouragement. Not even a goodbye.

I turned on my brights and peered as far ahead as the light went, then glanced at both of my side-view mirrors. I was hoping that Jesus was lurking around the truck, ready to hop back in. He wasn't.

I was on my own. Again.

I looked at the clock. 4:20. The hospital was an hour and a quarter away. There wasn't anything left to do but drive. Whatever Jesus had wanted to show me, he had shown me. Now I had to assimilate it.

I got out of the U-Haul to look at the damage on the side. It wasn't pretty. I hopped back in and pulled onto the highway. The truck was the least of my concerns.

I said a brief prayer for Mattie and the baby. *Let them be okay, Lord. Get us through this.* I had to pray—it's what Christians are supposed to do—but it still felt rote at best. Did God really care about what was happening to Mattie? One minute I got the news that the pregnancy was in trouble, and the next minute—no, faster than that—Jesus was gone.

Why would Jesus bail on me like that? Was he trying to teach me to trust him? Ride with me part of the way to Cincinnati, give me an illustration of God's love, then disappear to see if I'd believe it strongly enough?

Then the thought came to me: he's gone to be with Mattie, to take care of that situation. I felt a surge of hope. Jesus left when he did so that . . .

That train of thought slowed to a halt. Jesus knew beforehand about Mattie's situation. He didn't have to wait for a phone call. Why would he leave to be with her at precisely that moment? Besides, if he was leaving to be with Mattie, wouldn't he have said so? Why keep it a secret?

I couldn't assume anything about where Jesus had gone. He had simply vanished. That's all I knew for sure. I was on my own to make sense of all I'd seen and heard and to somehow integrate it into my life.

The more pavement my tires traversed, the more irritated I got. Fine, God loves me like the ocean. Jump in and you get all wet. That's what this whole night was turning into—all wet. First my dad ragged me out about my work, then I stormed out (why wasn't Jesus living through me then?), and Jesus climbed aboard and gave me and Larry this vision of our new selves, which was great. But honestly, what good was having a new self when everything was turning to crap? My new self couldn't do a thing about what I really cared about: our new baby. That was in the hands of someone who supposedly loved me perfectly. And had just bailed on me.

Maybe I was just giving in to my flesh. But how was I supposed to live in dependence on Jesus when he seemed anything but dependable? Twenty minutes before, I had a glimpse, at least, of how God loved me. I'd felt more of a connection to him. But now what?

My mind kept telling me, "You need to believe! You need to believe!" I was too hacked off to believe. Whatever trusting Christ in me looked like, I didn't feel capable of pulling it off at the moment. Whatever high I experienced from being with Jesus again had disappeared. Reality had hit me square in the face. The best I could now do was show up at the hospital and be there for Mattie. A spiritual white knight she wouldn't get. Not tonight.

I passed a mileage sign. Cincinnati 63. At least the construction had ended—not that it mattered much after the fact.

The miles passed. My anger slowly subsided into resignation. I'd had another encounter with Jesus. It's what I had wanted. It just didn't turn out as I had expected. Surely Jesus knew what would happen tonight. Our time together had to have a purpose. But in light of Mattie's call, even my glimpse into the realm of spirit seemed insufficient.

As I inched closer to Cincinnati, my encounter with Jesus took a back seat in my thoughts to Mattie. She had sounded so desperate on the phone. How serious was the bleeding? Was the pregnancy in jeopardy? The visual image of Mattie's last sonogram kept returning to me. The baby was so small. Twenty-six weeks. Would she live? And if so, would we face months of intensive neonatal care? What effect would that have on us? If the baby died, what effect would that have on our family? Our marriage? My faith in God?

I couldn't go there. I couldn't contemplate that we might lose the baby.

Lord, keep her alive. Do whatever it takes for this pregnancy to continue.

I increased my speed. If I got a ticket, I got a ticket.

Despite my anxiety, for the first time during the night, I began to feel sleepy. I had, after all, been up for twenty-two hours. I reached down to the floorboard and grabbed my box of Cheez-Its. How long would these keep me going? Despite my urgency to get to the hospital, I might have to stop and get some coffee to go.

Traffic picked up as I got within fifty miles of Cincinnati. I pulled up behind a car in the right-hand lane. I switched to the left lane to pass it. Just ahead was an SUV that, as I approached, seemed to be slowing. *Why are you slowing in the left-hand lane, you idiot?* I was about to move to the right when the SUV began veering gently to the left, toward the shoulder. *What is this person doing? You don't pull off to the left!* But the vehicle continued curving.

Then it occurred to me: the driver had fallen asleep.

I laid on my horn just as the SUV drifted off the shoulder and onto the grass median. Its brake lights came on. It decelerated abruptly and spun to the left. *I don't have time to deal with this!* But I had to help. I hit my brakes and pulled off on the shoulder, passing the vehicle as it came to a stop. Several hundred feet later, I hopped out of the U-Haul and jogged back to the SUV. The median was muddy from the thunderstorms that had passed through Friday night.

I ran around to the driver's side and looked through the window. The driver was a woman whom I guessed was around sixty. She looked disoriented, as if she was trying to get her bearings. I knocked lightly on the window.

She jerked around, startled.

"Are you okay?" I asked in a loud voice, exaggerating my lip movements.

She nodded.

"Do you need any help?"

She looked down at the electronic panel beside her and rolled the window down a few inches, giving me a better look at her. I stared in disbelief.

"Mrs. Miller?"

Chapter Eleven

ANNE MILLER WAS the leader of a Bible study Mattie attended and was the spiritual mentor of many women in our church. Mattie thought she hung the moon. "I can't tell you how much she's meant to my spiritual growth, Nick," she had told me numerous times. I saw her at the church sometimes, plus once a year when she and her husband invited the Bible study women and their husbands over for a barbeque. I had never talked with her one-on-one, however.

"Nick? What are you doing out here?"

"Heading back to Cincinnati. Did you fall asleep?"

"I . . . I must have." She glanced over her shoulder toward the road. "I think I'll be okay. I'll . . . um . . . Thanks so much for stopping." She managed a slight smile.

"You're welcome."

"Let me make sure I can pull this back on the road."

She put the SUV in reverse. I stepped away from the car. She accelerated but only spun the wheels. I couldn't see the ground, but I could hear the tires against the mud. She tried again. The vehicle spun slightly to the right but didn't make any progress.

"You're in the mud," I shouted. "I don't think you can drive out."

She looked at me, then tried one more time. It was useless. She turned the engine off. I walked back to the door. "Do you want me to call a tow truck?"

"How long do you think that might take?"

I shrugged. "The closest twenty-four-hour tow is probably on the outskirts of Cincinnati. AAA would know. Are you a member?"

"Yes, we are."

"If there's a truck immediately available, it might take half an hour to get here, ten minutes or so to pull you out."

She looked at the clock on her dashboard. "Okay."

"Do you have your AAA card?"

She reached into her purse and retrieved it.

"I'll call them for you. I'll be back in a minute."

I walked toward the U-Haul. I wasn't sorry to help Mrs. Miller, but why had God put this in my path now of all times?

I grabbed my Blackberry and called AAA en route back to the SUV. I talked for a minute while standing next to Mrs. Miller's vehicle and then lowered the phone. "They say they can have a truck here in an hour and a half."

"I don't think that leaves me enough time. I need to be at Bethesda North Hospital before 7:00."

Bethesda North. That was forty-five minutes past Good Samaritan, round trip. I had to get to Mattie! This night was getting worse by the minute. I glanced up the interstate, then back at her. "I . . . uh . . . I could drive you into Cincinnati now. You could come back for the car later today."

Her face brightened. "Would you? That's so kind of you, Nick." She leaned over, picked up her purse, and slid out of the car. "I hope this isn't too much trouble for you."

"No. I just . . . I need to get to a hospital myself, actually."

I motioned toward the U-Haul. We walked toward it.

"A relative?" she asked.

"Mattie. She started bleeding during the night."

"Oh." She stopped and put her hand on my arm. "Are she and the baby okay?"

"I don't know yet. She went to Good Samaritan. I haven't heard anything."

"Then you should go straight to her. Take me to Good Samaritan and I'll get a taxi from there. That'll still get me to Bethesda North in time."

Her offer came as a relief. We got in the truck and I pulled back onto the interstate. I glanced over at Anne. She seemed awfully calm.

"You don't seem all that upset about what happened back there."

She pushed her hand through the front of her hair. "Is that how it looks? I feel like a tornado swept through my insides. That was pretty harrowing—waking up while driving off the road. I was always in good hands, though."

"But you could have been killed."

She smiled. "Not unless Father had finished getting ready for me."

That was something Jesus might say. Was it possible Jesus had hopped back into my U-Haul? Could he—would he—disguise himself as someone I knew?

I dismissed the thought. Even after all I had experienced this evening, that still seemed far-fetched.

I was about to ask Anne a question when she asked one herself. "So how are you doing with Mattie going to the hospital?"

"Anxious. Mattie was pretty upset when she called. We had two miscarriages before this."

"Mattie told me." She paused for a moment. "Have you picked out a name for the baby?"

"We were thinking about Delaney. We haven't decided on a middle name yet."

"That's a beautiful name."

We rode in silence for a few moments. It was odd, riding in a U-Haul with Mattie's spiritual mentor. She probably knew more about Mattie's spiritual life than I did. Suddenly it occurred to me that if anyone could help answer a question I had asked Jesus, it was she.

"Mrs. Miller—"

"Please, call me Anne. Mrs. Miller is my mother."

"Okay. Anne. Can I ask you something?"

"Of course."

As I formulated the question in my mind, it suddenly seemed silly and hopelessly self-focused. But I couldn't help it. I wanted an answer. "This may sound like a strange question, but do you have any idea why Mattie seems to have grown a lot more spiritually than I have the last few years?"

"How do you know you haven't been growing?"

"I'm not saying I haven't been growing"—although, as far as I could tell, that was the truth. "But it seems Mattie has grown more. She seems much closer to God."

"God's already brought all of us as close as we can get," she replied, "but I know what you mean. Mattie hasn't told you enough herself for you to answer that?"

I shook my head. "We don't talk about spiritual things all that much. She tries from time to time. But I guess—well actually, I know—I'm usually too discouraged to talk about my spiritual life."

She was silent. I added, "I'm not asking you to reveal anything about Mattie that she wouldn't say herself."

"No, I understand." She shifted in her seat so that her body was facing more towards me. "After Mattie met Jesus six years ago on the airplane—"

"She told you about that?"

"Yes." She looked surprised that I would expect otherwise. "It's an important part of her story. She told me about you meeting Jesus too."

"And you believed her?"

"I didn't have a reason not to. Besides, Mattie seemed too innocent about the religious world to make up something."

That was the truth. But I couldn't believe Mattie had told Anne, or that Anne believed her. I wished I could have had a friend or mentor like that all these years.

"Go on," I said.

"Whenever I mentor someone, I make sure they're grounded in two things. These are the two that have been most important to me. But Mattie already had the first."

"Which was what?"

"She was already enthralled with Jesus. We have to have that. He has to captivate our hearts. God the Father is enthralled with his Son. We have to be enthralled too, so that we want Jesus to have the supremacy in everything, just as the Father does. Weren't you enthralled with Jesus after you met him?"

"Yes," I admitted.

"So was Mattie when I met her. It wasn't that long after she had met Jesus personally, and I could tell that about her. I just wanted to help her stay that way."

"And how did she do that?" My real question was, *how could I do that?*

"By spending time with him in the Word and truly focusing on him—not on what she should do, but just on him. And also by training herself to see him in everything. All things are from him, and through him, and to him. If our eyes are on him and how wonderful he is, he will take care of the *do's*. That's what he promises."

That's what Jesus had told me earlier: God himself would cause us to express his character.

Hearing Anne say these things out loud, I immediately recognized their reality in Mattie's life. Unlike me, she really had continued to be enthralled with Jesus.

I brought my focus back to Anne. "And what's the second thing you teach the women?"

"I teach them that they are part of Jesus."

It took a second for her words to sink in. I wasn't sure if I had heard her right.

"You teach them what?"

"That they are part of Jesus."

I thought what Jesus had said earlier was radical. I wasn't sure I even wanted to know where this was leading.

Chapter Twelve

TRAFFIC SLOWED AS we passed the "Entering Cincinnati" sign. A house trailer ahead was occupying a lane and a half of the freeway's three lanes. I had to focus on the road a moment. It gave me time to regroup.

Among some at our church, Anne Miller had the reputation of being rather out there, of pushing the theological envelope. I had always dismissed the rumors as unfounded; Mattie never had any concerns. Now, for the first time, I wondered whether the rumors were justified.

Had Mattie fallen all these years under the influence of questionable teaching? I had seen the positive fruit in Mattie's life, but did she need to distance herself from these roots? This claim of being "part of Jesus" made me incredibly uncomfortable.

It dawned on me, however, that perhaps Anne was only saying what Jesus had stated earlier in the evening.

"You mean you're joined to him," I replied.

"Well, yes, and so are you."

I breathed a little easier. Maybe I wouldn't have to consult the pastoral staff about her after all.

"I learned that for the first time to—" I was about to say *tonight*, but I thought better of it. How could I explain what I had learned without mentioning how I had learned it? At this point, I didn't want to delve into my second meeting with Jesus, especially since it had ended so poorly. "Fairly recently," I said.

"You did? That's wonderful. Did Mattie share that with you?"

"Not really. Well, she may have, but if so it didn't sink in."

"Father uses all sorts of instruments. The important thing is that you realize it now. Most Christians never do. For me, realizing I was part of Jesus made him even more real."

There were those uncomfortable words again. Maybe she was a heretic after all. "I guess I'm not quite ready to say that about myself."

She smiled. "You don't have to. God already says it."

My brow furrowed. "He does? Where?"

"He says we are members of his body."

"But that just means we're part of the universal church."

"It means much more than that." She spoke confidently, calmly, as if she knew the truth and didn't need to win an argument. "Aren't the members of your body part of you?"

"Of course, but the New Testament just uses that language as a metaphor. Jesus does his work on earth through the church, the body."

She shook her head softly. "God uses that language because it reflects spiritual reality."

Those were words Jesus had used earlier: there were spiritual realities I hadn't accounted for, he said.

Anne continued. "He doesn't say we are *like* Christ's body. He says we *are* Christ's body. We are members of him. Why do you think Jesus said to Paul, 'Why are you persecuting me?' when Paul was persecuting the church? It's because Jesus doesn't see the church, or its members, as separate from himself. We're one with him. We're part of him now."

I glanced in my side-view mirror and moved into the middle lane to pass a car, all the while thinking about her statement. "I don't know. I just don't see where the Bible states that directly."

"How about this: 'For even as the body is one and yet has many members, and all the members of the body though they are many, are one body, so also is Christ.'"

"That just says the Body of Christ operates like a human body."

"No, you didn't hear it right. Almost no one does the first time." She repeated the verse. "Paul isn't comparing the Body of Christ to a human body; he's comparing *Christ* to a human body. As the body has many members, so also does Christ. Christ has made himself a corporate being. You are part of that being. So am I."

"Say the verse again."

She repeated it again. She was right.

"So are you saying there's no distinction between Jesus and us?" I asked.

"No. Jesus is God. We aren't. That will never change. But he has brought us into himself and made us one with him—an actual part of himself."

I was trying to wrap my mind around the concept,

which seemed even more mind-boggling than being joined to Jesus. "But everything we do is not Jesus," I objected. "When I sin, it's not Jesus sinning through me."

"True. But when you sin, you take Jesus there with you. That's what he told the Corinthians. Don't take the members of Christ and join them to a prostitute."

I sat silently, trying to process the implications of what she was saying. Maybe she was right. Maybe Jesus did see us as part of himself. If I was now a part of Jesus . . . "So you're saying God doesn't even see my sin when he looks at me. He just sees Jesus."

"Yes, because you're part of him. He only sees his Son. He is completely enthralled by his Son. He sees his Son being expressed by you."

"But surely God isn't blind to my sin."

"No, of course not. But it's not the ultimate reality to him. He knows it's temporary. He uses its consequences to train you."

I thought about the episode earlier in the evening with my dad. "Okay, so I'm just thinking out loud, all right?"

"All right."

"I had this bad scene with my dad in Chicago."

"What happened?"

I was embarrassed to admit what I had done, but Anne seemed as accepting as a person could be. "He kept getting on my case about my career, which he does sometimes, and I ended up stomping out and driving away tonight, instead of in the morning like I had planned."

She smiled. "It seems God planned something different."

"If what you're saying is true, then when my dad was saying those things, he wasn't saying them to me alone. He was saying them to Jesus and me."

"That's right. You don't exist independently anymore. You are part of Jesus. Anything that comes to you comes to him."

I thought about that for a moment. "And he is capable of responding in a loving way, isn't he?"

She nodded. "Always."

"So why didn't I respond in a loving way?"

"Because you still have free will. Your union with Christ—it's a partnership. He lives through us, but he doesn't force it on us."

"So how do I get him to live through me more?"

I had become so engrossed in our conversation that I almost missed the exit for Good Samaritan. I crossed two lanes and got off the freeway. We stopped at a light on the access road. I turned to Anne again. "How do I get him to do that?"

She gave a slight laugh. "Well, we can't force him to do anything, can we? But he's chosen to live through us. He does that more as we train ourselves to see as he sees: to see beyond the external to the unseen reality."

"Which means what, exactly?"

"To me, it means three things. First, that I see Christ in everything."

"In everything?"

"The Bible tells us that. It says he is over all and through all and in all. He fills all in all. It says that he who descended is also the one who ascended far above all the heavens, so that he might fill all things. Everything in the universe is an expression of him."

"But not evil. Not sin."

She nodded. "Everything is not a perfect expression of him. Not yet. But one day it will be. In the meantime, by faith we choose to see him. I look at myself, I see him. I lived for so long with my eyes on myself—how I was doing, how I was measuring up. But I was never good enough. It seems like that's where you've been."

"Exactly," I said as I turned onto Martin Luther King Drive.

"Looking at yourself is never walking by faith. You are not the life within you. He is."

"But I always see me messing up."

She smiled. "Faith is not sight. It is the assurance of things *not* seen. We choose to see him and him only. We are expressions of him. And he is always adequate. He is always perfect. As we walk in that faith, he expresses himself through us more fully."

We stopped at a light. The first rays of sunlight reflected back from office buildings, announcing the arrival of a new day.

"Likewise," Anne continued. "I choose to see only him in others."

"But what if they don't know him?"

"In some way, everyone expresses him. Either Christ is being formed within them, or he has kept them in disobedience that he may show mercy to all, as Paul says. By faith, I choose to see all as expressions of him. Just as I see every circumstance as an expression of him. All situations are God coming to me in different forms. I see him in everything."

Seeing Christ in everything. That was the opposite of how I lived. When I looked at me, I saw only me. When I looked at those around me, I saw . . . annoying people. When I looked at my circumstances, I saw only hassles.

"You're saying choose to see Christ in spite of what's actually there."

She laughed. "No, Nick. I'm saying see Christ because he is what's actually there. He fills all in all. I can either live in that reality, or I can live by what my physical eyes see. I choose to live in God's reality."

We turned on Dixmyth Avenue.

"You said there were three things," I said.

"I did. The second is this: God doesn't expect me to do it."

I glanced at her. "Do what?"

"Whatever he instructs us to do. All the commands of the Bible."

"You're saying he expects us to ignore what he says?"

"No. I'm saying that I'm not the one he expects to accomplish them."

That sounded counterintuitive, but I recalled what Jesus had said, that there are no rules. Is this what he meant? "Then who does he expect to do it?" I asked.

"His Son. We have to remember that we are containers of him. He created us to live through us. Now, having done that, he's hardly going to turn around and ask us to try to live the life on our own, is he? But that's how most Christians try to live."

She was right about that.

"You see," she said, "the minute I expect myself to do it, I've put myself under law. 'I have to do this and do it right.' Love my husband. Love my children. Love my neighbor. Love my enemies. Rejoice in trials. Be perfect, as he is perfect. Who can do that?"

"I certainly can't."

"Neither can I. And if I place that burden on myself, I have placed myself under law, and that leads to self-effort and failure. Because that's not how God created us to operate."

This was starting to make sense. "So instead of expecting myself to do it . . ."

"I trust Christ to do it," she answered. "That's number three. I look only to him in me. Only he can live God's life. That's what God's commands are—a description of his life. But only he can live it. He made us to be containers of him, that he might live it through us. Our role is faith—looking only to him to do it."

I stopped at another light. The hospital was in the next block.

"So it's not 'what would Jesus do,'" I said.

She shook her head. "Not at all. It's 'what will Jesus do.' Through us, he walks into every circumstance. We may not like being there. We may not feel loving, or kind, or patient. I often don't. But Jesus is complete other-love. He always does what is best for the other. So I stop and say, 'Jesus, what are you going to do here?' I'm completely available for him to live through. And he loves in the way he wants—often to my complete surprise."

"You're saying faith is the key."

"I'm saying Jesus is the key. Faith puts the key in the door. I found that when I first started learning about Christ in me, it was still about me—me trying to let him live through me. Even living by faith can be about us. But one day God showed me that because I'm part of Christ, he's my point of reference. And I could simply fix my eyes on him. When I taught myself to do that consistently, it's amazing how I saw him living through me. And how much I was at rest on the inside. He is all, and he's all I need in every situation."

I pulled into the parking lot, cut the engine, and

reached for the door handle. Then I turned toward Anne. "When I got the call from Mattie earlier, I thought Jesus had abandoned me."

"Jesus can't abandon you, Nick. You're a part of him."

I let that stay with me a moment. "You know, a little while ago, I thought for a minute that maybe you were Jesus."

She laughed and shook her head. "Well, I never confuse myself with him, that's for sure. Besides, last time I checked, Jesus wasn't a woman."

"Well, there's that book in which God the Father is an African-American woman."

"I read it. Trust me, I'm definitely not Jesus." She placed her hand gently on my arm. "But he was here, wasn't he? In both of us."

She glanced toward the front of the hospital where two taxis were parked. "Well, I'd better get over to Bethesda North, and you'd better go see Mattie."

We got out of the truck and walked across the parking lot.

"Anne, could you be praying for Mattie and Delaney?"

"I have been, Nick, ever since we got in your truck. Father has them in his hands."

Suddenly I realized I had been so focused on my own situation that I had never asked about hers. "Why do you have to be at the hospital?"

"Vern is having emergency bypass surgery."

"This morning? Why didn't you say so? And how can you be so calm about it?"

She shook her head. "I'm not really so calm. My feelings have been a roller coaster. But I always come back to this: my husband is a part of Jesus, and so am I. And nothing happens to his members that Jesus doesn't allow."

We walked to a taxi and I held the door open for Anne. She slid in, then leaned her head back out. "I've enjoyed our time together, Nick. Jesus was living through you, getting me here."

I felt a smile cross my face. "He was, wasn't he? I've enjoyed it too, Anne."

She reached for the door and then looked up at me again. "Become enthralled with Jesus, Nick. He is all. He'll show you how. He always does."

She closed the door and waved at me as the taxi drove off. I thought for a moment about her final words before my mind shifted back to the here and now. I needed to find Mattie. But even that immediate reality, I realized, had somehow changed.

I entered the hospital and went to the front desk. Mattie, I was told, was on the fourth floor. I walked briskly to the elevator bay and rode up. I exited, glanced around, and saw a large sign that said "Labor and Delivery." I strode toward the double doors. As I did, I passed a waiting area. It was deserted save for one man reading a magazine. Out of the corner of my eye I thought the face seemed familiar. I turned for a better look.

It was Jesus.

My whole body relaxed. With Jesus here, it was impossible not to immediately feel at ease. Whatever was happening with Mattie and the baby, Jesus would make sure it turned out all right.

I reflexively took a step toward him.

Then I stopped.

Like scales falling from my eyes, it all became clear. This time, Jesus' physical presence was a test, a learning experience. Was I willing, by faith, to put into practice what he had been teaching me all night? Or would I revert to my prior understanding of reality—the understanding

I possessed, unbelievably, merely hours before as I left Chicago?

Time froze as I took the moment in. Before he went to the cross, Jesus had told the disciples he was leaving. They were distraught, but he told them something they couldn't grasp: it was to their advantage that he leave. Only then could he return to live inside them and live his life through them.

Now I was in the place of the disciples. Jesus was giving me a choice, a choice for this one moment: would I insist on his physical presence, or would I trust his indwelling presence? Would I see only the outward, or would I see through to the deeper reality? Would I be like the disciples before the resurrection, or would I be like Paul, seeing that Christ is all and in all?

Jesus lowered the magazine and looked at me. Our eyes met. In our previous meetings, I had seen in those eyes love, wisdom, understanding. Now I saw something else. I saw myself in them. I was a part of him. He was the life in me. Though always distinct, we were one.

Something else became clear as well. Jesus had left earlier, not to desert me, but to teach me what I could only learn away from his physical presence. He didn't abandon me. He could never abandon me.

I nodded gently to him. My lips parted and I spoke loudly enough for him to hear across the room. "Thank you."

He smiled. "You're welcome, Nick."

I motioned with my head toward the door. "Let's go in, shall we?"

He nodded. "Let's go in."

I left him in the waiting room as I turned and walked through the doors.

Author's Note

If you are intrigued by the message of "Christ in us" as presented in *Night with a Perfect Stranger*, I invite you to check into a book I coauthored with pastor Dan Stone called *The Rest of the Gospel: When the Partial Gospel Has Worn You Out*. It more fully explores how to experience the reality of Christ as the life within us. *The Rest of the Gospel* is available at davidgregorybooks.com or on Amazon.

David Gregory is the author of the *New York Times* Extended Bestseller *Dinner with a Perfect Stranger*, as well as *A Day with a Perfect Stranger*, *The Next Level*, *The Last Christian*, and coauthor of *The Rest of the Gospel*. After a ten-year business career, David earned master's degrees from Dallas Theological Seminary and the University of North Texas. He now writes full-time and lives in the Pacific Northwest.

WORTHY
PUBLISHING

IF YOU LIKED THIS BOOK...

- Tell your friends by going to: http://www.nightwith aperfectstranger.com and clicking "LIKE"

- Share the video book trailer by posting it on your Facebook page

- Head over to our Facebook page, click "LIKE" and post a comment regarding what you enjoyed about the book

- Tweet "I recommend reading #NightWithAPerfectStranger by David Gregory @Worthypub"

- Hashtag: #NightWithAPerfectStranger

- Subscribe to our newsletter by going to http://worthypublishing.com/about/subscribe.php

WORTHY PUBLISHING
FACEBOOK PAGE

WORTHY PUBLISHING
WEBSITE